Boxing - From Chump to Champ 2

An Advanced 7 Step Boxing Manual.

Discover how to Develop Discipline, Become Fighting Fit, and Improve Your Boxing Ability to Win in the Ring.

Andrew Hudson

The data, depictions, events, descriptions, and all other information forthwith are considered to be true, fair, and accurate unless the work is expressly described as a work of fiction. Regardless of the nature of this work, the Publisher is exempt from any responsibility of actions taken by the reader in conjunction with this work. The Publisher acknowledges that the reader acts of their own accord and releases the author and Publisher of any responsibility for the observance of tips, advice, counsel, strategies, and techniques that may be offered in this volume.

Table of Contents

Table of Contents....................................5

Introduction..8

How I Can Help You..11

Chapter 1: #1 Building a Strong Foundation.. 21

Let's Revisit a Few Things..........................22

What's Your Style? 30

Developing a Chin 57

Chapter 2: #2 How to Get Seriously Fit for Boxing...65

What to Know Before Your First Boxing Workout..67

Increase Your Stamina and Strength..........69

Strengthening Your Midsection.................81

The Pugilist's Diet 87

Bernard Hopkin's Diet 95

Floyd Mayweather's Diet...........................96

Chapter 3: #3 Practise Advanced Techniques for Successful Boxing.......99

Advanced Punching Techniques................99

Advanced Punching Combinations for the Heavy Bag...113

Shadowboxing 117

Benefits of Shadowboxing 122
The Stance Switch 127
Shifts of Attack 133
Various Drills 136
Chapter 4: #4 Training 1-on-1 for Excellent Fighting Experience 144
Focus Mitt Drills.. 147
Sparring 162
Improving Reaction Time and Agility 173
Chapter 5: #5 Further Boxing Tips and Tricks 183
The Clinch 183
Conserving Energy 187
Fighting with a Low Guard 191
Fighting in a Low Stance 193
Common Boxing Combinations to Try During Sparring 194
More Important Advice............................ 195
Chapter 6: #6 Winning the Mental Battle 199
Training Your Brain 201
Practicing Mindfulness 204
Setting Goals 213
Overtraining 216

Chapter 7: #7 Additional Defensive Techniques and How to Return a Punch 220

Layers of Defense 221

Boxing Guards 224

Countering Different Punches 229

Baiting Your Opponent 232

Forcing the Counter 236

Chapter 8: How to Successfully Take Your Skills to the Ring 239

Getting Involved in Competition 240

What to Look For in a Boxing Coach 244

Start Your Goal Setting 247

Boxing is a Metaphor for Life 249

Conclusion 256

References..260

Introduction

Imagine being a young child growing up in a rough neighborhood. Every day that you walk out of your front door, you are terrified of what you might encounter. You always try to remain under the radar, so bullies will not pick on you. Most of the time, this strategy works. However, what will you do if you get caught? At this point, it's either time to try and outrun your bullies, stand and take whatever they give you, or fight back.

Picture yourself surrounded by scary individuals who are physically more prominent than you and you have no clue what you will do next. This would be a frightening scenario to be in. On the other hand, consider how good it would feel if you remained calm, composed, and confident because you know you can defend yourself. Furthermore, if you end up throwing hands, you will do very well. Why is this? Because, in the latter scenario, you took boxing lessons.

Boxing is a sport that is appreciated around the world, not only because it gives people the ability to defend themselves but also improves confidence, energy, and fitness. It is also fun to watch an exciting fight on television or in person. There is a wealth of other benefits, as well. Boxing is a great sport because it increases physical strength and stamina while also teaching strategy. The sport is called the sweet science for a reason, and as you learn more about the various techniques, defensive and offensive maneuvers, footwork, and body movement, etc., you will understand why.

I recognize that many of you out there are afraid to stand up for yourself. You are worried that you will get hurt and look foolish if you do. I completely feel your pain in this regard. Also, you may have tried various exercises and either did not enjoy them or received no benefits from them. Once again, I recognize how you feel, and that's why I want to help you.

When you develop your boxing prowess, you will gain immense confidence in what you are capable of. The days of getting pushed around will soon go by the wayside because you will steadily improve your physical and mental strength. As a result, you will become more courageous in every aspect of life. Furthermore, you get to engage in a fun workout that brings tremendous results. The sport of boxing works out more than your arms. After every session, you will feel like every section of your body, from head-to-toe, was targeted.

If you have followed me in the past, then you probably remember the prequel to this book, which was part 1. My objective here is to expand on that knowledge and information and present more ways on how boxing can change your life and circumstances. While the first book was starting at the beginner level, this book is a step up from that. After you are done and begin incorporating what I teach you, there will be a noticeable gain in your boxing ability. You will also find yourself getting fit with the exercises I go over.

One of the greatest things about boxing is that it can be done anywhere. All you need is a big enough space to move around, and if you aren't too self-conscious, you can even go to a park to practice. I will go over many advanced training methods that you can add to your beginner level repertoire. You can slowly begin moving towards becoming an expert, which is actually a lifelong pursuit.

In addition to solo exercises, I will also discuss the different types of equipment to help you further with your skills and also discuss the idea of sparring. Having a partner or two can significantly help with your skill level. When you begin to learn the techniques and strategies I go over in this book, my suspicion is that you will want to begin sparring with someone. Training on your own is great but has its limits. Having someone to provide resistance will make you even better. You will be able to practice your punches, footwork, defensive skills, and various other boxing techniques with another person. This will make you a next level competitor.

Once you have completed this book, the ball will be in your court. From there, you can decide which direction you want to go. One thing I can ensure is that whatever path you decide to take, you will do it with more confidence and discipline. I have no doubt that you can achieve great boxing skills and get in amazing shape by doing so. At the very least, you will always have a fun activity to engage in.

What I do not encourage is using the skills I teach you to become a bully to others. My hope is that you will take the teachings I provide and use them in a positive way. That includes not using it to harm others intentionally. Always remember that if you must use these skills, it can only be for self-defense and not to create problems on purpose. I have faith that all of you will follow this advice.

How I Can Help You

Before we get any further, let me introduce myself. My name is Andrew Hudson, and I have been a boxing coach and personal trainer for many years. I have been studying boxing for eight years and have taught many people. My hope is that you read the prequel to this book and are returning for more because you enjoyed the information that was imparted. I have benefited in many ways by incorporating the sweet science into my life, and I want to help as many other people as I can learn the sport I love and get into great shape while doing so.

Sadly, as I look around, I see so many people who do not engage in any physical activity and eat nothing but junk. This has led to so many people becoming overweight and having to deal with chronic illnesses, even at a young age. I find this horrid and have set out a goal to change that. Perhaps people do not know how much fun boxing is. They might have watched it on television and see no appeal in trying to bash someone else's head in. Well, after working with me, their mindsets usually change, which makes me happy.

I want to continue getting people involved in boxing by showing them the many fun sides, like circuit training, shadowboxing, hitting the mitts, and heavy bag training. When I watched my past students, many of whom never trained in boxing before, greatly improve their skills, obtain a better physique, and walk around with more confidence, I knew that my job was done. My success is determined by how much value I can bring to my clients, and I want to do this for you.

There are only so many people I can teach in a class or one-on-one session. I believe that this book will reach many more people who will gain an advantage with my teachings. The reason I want to help so many individuals is that I know what it's like to be a beginner. I know what it's like to not be in shape, have zero self-esteem, and always worry about being picked on. I was there, just like so many of you. It was a blessing for me that I found boxing, and I want to bestow it on others. I look forward to sharing my knowledge and experience with all of you. Thank you for continuing on your boxing and fitness path with me. Let's get started on improving your skills!

Your Free Gift

The gift you will receive is "The Basic Boxing Bundle". In this bundle you will find many 'extras' that will help you improve your boxing ability in many ways. In this bundle you will find...

An equipment checklist – a page that has all the equipment mentioned in this book in a list with a link to where you can find it for a reasonable price on a website. Although all the equipment is not needed it certainly will help you improve.

Secondly, you will find 5 Boxing Drills that you can complete at home. Each drill is different to help develop certain aspects of your boxing game, one thing they all have in common is that they get you working hard. The drills are detailed and essential for improvement.

Finally, you will find a Boxing Video Hub. I believe that these videos are helpful for learning correct form and each video in the Hub is labelled so that you know what boxing video you are clicking on.

Follow this link:

https://hudsonandrew.activehosted.com/f/1

Join the Chump to Champ Community

Boxing on your own is difficult because it requires you to motivate yourself to train on a regular basis, motivating yourself is much more challenging that having a coach shout in your ear to finish your reps. Training on your own is very beneficial because it allows you to make the training specific to you so that you can work on your own schedule and improve the parts of your boxing that suits your style. That's why you should join the Chump to Champ Community.

In this Free Facebook Community, you will be able to discover much more information about boxing because I post twice a day. These posts consist of beginner information, debunking myths, providing links to videos for your benefit, many boxing trivia questions and so much more for your entertainment and benefit. Not to mention there are many other members in this community in your position, anyone can contribute in any way they like and if you join please make a post about yourself to feel welcomed by the other members

Follow this link to join the Chump to Champ Community:

https://www.facebook.com/groups/chumptochamp

Free Boxing from Chump to Champ 2 eBook

You may find that in this book there are a few links for you to follow which is inconvenient because you can follow a link through a paperback book without spending 10 minutes typing in 40-character links into your URL.

The links in this book are beneficial to help you progress further with your boxing ability and I don't want you to miss out on them. That is why I am giving you the free PDF eBook copy of this book so that you can access all the links with just a click.

To get the eBook, you will have to type in a short link into your URL (ironic I know...) and you will have the eBook emailed directly to your inbox.

So please type this short link into your internet browser to have easier access to links in this book:

https://hudsonandrew.activehosted.com/f/21

Health Check

Before you start this fitness routine - please consult with your doctor.

- Do not attempt to exercise while unwell.
- Do not carry-on exercising if you feel pain - if the pain doesn't calm please tell your doctor.
- Avoid exercising after consuming alcohol or a large meal within the last couple of hours.
- If you take prescribed medication, check with your doctor to make sure it is okay to exercise.
- If you are in any doubt, go check with a doctor. It may be helpful to show the doctor the training routines you will partake in, if the doctor suggests for you not to partake in certain exercises there are always alternatives that will suit you.

Think before you train. If you are under 16 years old, then I advise you to stay away from lifting weights as your body hasn't fully developed. I 'Andrew Hudson' will not take any responsibility for any physical injuries caused by exercises I have stated in this book – injuries are a part of fitness and can always be avoided so please train responsibly.

Read through the entire book before performing any of the circuits/warmups/cooldowns.

Chapter 1: #1 Building a Strong Foundation

Are you excited about improving your boxing ability? Well, let's slow down a little bit. Before going any further, did you read part one of this series? If the answer is no, I urge you to go back and do so. The starting point of this book is where the other book left off. Therefore, I am not starting from scratch here, and if you are still a novice, the information may go right over your head. Much of the terminology and information will not be gone into with great detail since I went over it in part one. For example, specific punches will not be described again.

If you did read part one, congratulations on continuing your journey with me. I am happy to have you back. As you started incorporating the information and training regimen from my first book into your routine, you probably noticed a lot of advancement in your skill and fitness. However, that was only the beginning. There are still countless boxing skills and training methods you will need to learn. In fact, even the most experienced boxers in the world have not learned everything. Those who think they do often have a sharp fall from grace.

Let's Revisit a Few Things

I do not want this book to be a complete recap of the first book. However, I do want to revisit a few topics before we move further along. Since this book is a continuation of part one, I always want you to remember the basics from the first book and continue to practice them. Never forget the basics, no matter how advanced you become with your skillset. These fundamentals will always serve as the foundation of your boxing skills. If you lose them, everything else will fall apart.

Stances and Footwork

In the first book, I detailed the importance of having a solid stance. Your stance is literally the starting point from where the remainder of your techniques are built off of. If you ignore this aspect, your balance, movement, footwork, defense, and even punching power will be affected. A boxer's stance is determined by several factors, like their size, arm length, and specific strengths and weaknesses.

The idea behind having a perfect body stance is that there is not one. This completely depends on the individual and what feels comfortable for them. If you watch many of the greats from the past or present, their stances are unique to their specific abilities. None are just like the other. This is why you should not just try to mimic the stance of a boxing expert. It takes time to develop a base you are comfortable with, and just copying someone else like a mirror image can cause you to miss out on the fundamentals.

Mike Tyson, George Foreman, Earnie Shavers, and Ray Mercer are considered some of the hardest-hitting heavyweights of all time. If you watch the way they stood in the ring, they will all look different because their styles, body structure, and movement, etc., were not the same. A good boxing stance will provide you with many different attributes, including:

- Power
- Defense
- Range
- Balance
- Flexibility

- Mobility
- Stability

A pugilist like the legendary Muhammad Ali was incredibly light on his feet. However, he also had great balance, stamina, and punching ability. He knew what worked for him and used it well. During Ali's prime, he was nearly impossible to hit, even when he stood right in front of a guy. There is a famous clip out there of Ali standing in the corner while his opponent is swarming him. Ali s simply ducking and dodging all of the blows.

Another legend in more modern times is Floyd Mayweather. He went 50-0 during his 21-year career and became famous for not taking punishment. He embodies the philosophy of "hit and don't get hit." One of the greatest defensive practitioners of all time, Mayweather knew how to stand, place his feet, and throw punches while giving his opponents virtually no target to hit back on. Looking back on his fight with Oscar De La Hoya, to the untrained eye, it seemed that De La Hoya, who was also great in his prime, was punishing Mayweather. However, if you look closely, most of his punches were either glancing blows or missing Mayweather completely. Ali and Mayweather had different stances but were both incredibly hard to hit.

To create a good boxing stance, you must pay attention to several things, like your foot placement and heel-toe alignment. This includes the distance between each foot, where your toes are pointed, and weight distribution over the foot. Also, you need to pay attention to how your upper body aligns with your lower body. When you fight, you fight with your whole body. When entering the boxing world, whatever your goal may be, your stance should be the first thing you focus on.

Defense in Boxing

Defensive skills are an especially important aspect of boxing because anytime you get hit, you are risking getting knocked out and severely injured. Once again, if you look at the greats, they all had varying ways of defending themselves. For example, Mike Tyson used the famous peek-a-boo style where he crouched down low, kept his hands high in front of his face, and used nonstop head movement at all times. Lennox Lewis, on the other hand, used his height and reach as an advantage.

There are numerous ways to defend against a strike:

- Bobbing and weaving where you are constantly moving your head up and down and side-to-side. This technique can disrupt an opponent's rhythm and open them up for strikes.
- Slipping is more of a reactionary defensive technique where you slip to the right or left when your opponent throws a punch.
- Parrying is where you deflect your opponent's punches with your hands, which can redirect their motion and body trajectory.
- Clinching is when you tie up your opponent, so your opponent cannot throw bombs on the inside.
- Rolling is when you twist or move your body away from the momentum of your opponent's punches.

I will get into all of these defensive techniques at a greater level in chapter seven.

Throwing a Good Punch

Of course, there is the most well-known aspect of boxing, and that is to throw good punches. In the end, winning a match will come down to who threw and landed the higher quality and quantity of punches. Some of the most common punches in boxing include:

- The jab
- The cross
- The overhand
- The hook
- The uppercut

When you master the ideas of stances, footwork, body mechanics, and defense, you will be able to throw some devastating punches from a variety of angles. When you combine everything, you will become a master of hitting and not getting hit.

I know I breezed through these topics, but I covered them in great detail in the first book. I urge you to revisit them frequently. My goal for the remainder of this book is to further improve your skills by going over several advanced methods and working on more drills. I hope you are ready for a fun ride!

What's Your Style?

By now, you have probably figured out what many of your strengths and weaknesses are. For example, do you have great balance and punching power but are smaller in stature? Are you tall and lanky? Are you more interested in the science of fighting or having brute force? Do you have a tough chin or a soft chin? Are you more aggressive or passive in your approach? Essentially, do you like to strike first or wait for the fight to come to you? There are no incorrect answers here. I just want you to understand yourself well so you can determine the best style to employ.

Styles make fights, and certain fighters can throw off their opponents simply because of their techniques. Their skills may not be more advanced, but they understand how to throw off certain opponents. The focus of this section will be to go over the various styles in boxing and what you might be the most comfortable with based on your unique attributes and shortcomings. When I say shortcomings, I do not mean to be disrespectful. Everyone has them, and your role as a boxer will be to recognize and work around them.

Pressure Fighter

A pressure fighter is one of the most entertaining boxers you will find. Whether you are a boxing fan or not, you will be enthralled by their aggression and destructive style. The goal of a pressure fighter is to swarm and overwhelm their opponents by moving forward constantly and throwing a barrage of punches. Manny Pacquiao, Mike Tyson, Joe Frazier, and Roberto Duran are all examples of legendary pressure fighters.

Of course, any bar brawler can throw a bunch of haymakers. To become a skilled and successful pressure fighter, you have to learn specific techniques to make it work for you. Otherwise, you will simply wear yourself out, barely do any damage to your opponent, and get taken out. If you are more of the aggressive type who likes to throw a lot of punches and essentially strike first, then you probably have more of the pressure fighter mindset. The following are some of the main qualities of this type of style:

- Putting constant pressure on an opponent and forcing him to react or back down.
- They are always moving around inside of the ring.
- They are always using counters quickly and effectively.
- They can wear down opponents by constantly staying on them.

After learning the techniques of boxing from the first book, you probably understand how exhausting it is to throw punches and move around the ring constantly. The various drills alone can empty out your gas tank. Now, imagine adding a person who is trying to take your head off. This is why it's important to focus on certain aspects of your style, so you can still put pressure on your opponent but conserve your energy at the same time. Therefore, I will go over some tactics to help you become a more efficient pressure fighter.

Cutting off the Ring

Cutting off the ring means you are skillfully forcing your opponent to remain in one section of the canvas to avoid having to expend too much energy trying to catch them. This is a major concern when a pressure fighter goes up against a boxer who knows how to move around the ring well. If you do not cut them off, they will tire you out. Once you run out of steam, your power, speed, and aggression will become useless. Let's look at a few points to help you master this skill:

- Walk down your opponent: Always keep your opponent directly in front of you and imagine they are in a small box. Try to keep them in this imaginary box and close in on them.

- If your opponent is in the corner, focus on keeping them inside an imaginary line. Watch them closely and as they move, sidestep with them while also closing in. You will basically be moving in a zigzag pattern. Work not to let your opponent get away from you. This means you have to watch them like a hawk.
- At some point, any decent boxer will be able to escape the corner. If they are along the ropes, once again, sidestep with them. Attempt to corner them again while doing this and keep your range until it is a good time to attack. Do not just run towards your opponent because they can simply move out of the way and use your own momentum against you as a matador does to a bull.

- Do not follow your opponent around the ring and make it obvious. You must be subtle in your approach and inch-in closer without them even realizing it. Never follow them in a straight line or circle because they will simply pivot and circle around you all day. Keep sidestepping with them and move in closer little by little. Don't give them an exit route.

Once you are in throwing range and have your opponent where you want them, you can now start throwing some heavy bombs. A good punch to utilize here is the hook. If your opponent attempts to get out of the corner, throw a hook from the arm in the direction they are moving. They will run into your arm, and you will become a nightmare for them.

Power

To be an effective pressure fighter, you need to have decent power. You don't need to be like Earnie Shavers, but you must be able to inflict significant damage and get your opponent's respect. They must become somewhat scared to engage with you; otherwise, they will run right over you with complete ease. The more power behind your punches, the quicker you can take a person out. Pressure fighters are not known for wanting to win on points. They look for the knockout! Overwhelm your opponent with hooks, crosses, and uppercuts. Use the jab to close distance but focus on the power punches to get the job done.

Working the Body

Go for the head when you can but do not always rely on being a headhunter, especially if your opponent has quick feet and good upper body movement. You will miss many of your punches and waste a lot of useful energy. Good pressure fighters are still strategic with the punches they throw. Instead of automatically going high, go for the body early and often. This will break down your opponent, and once the body falls, so will the head.

Think about chopping down a tree. When you do, are you throwing the axe up high or hitting the trunk at the base? Have this same mindset for body attacks.

Furthermore, when you target the body, your opponent will naturally bring their arms down, exposing their head. From here, you can start throwing some punches up high too. Even if you are getting outboxed, continue to invest in your body punches. It will pay off heavily in the end.

Combination Punching

A pressure fighter should not be throwing one punch at a time. While you don't want to waste energy throwing a bunch of haymakers just for the heck of it, you must put yourself in a position to throw multiple punches. Even if some don't land or get blocked, they can still create other openings. Throwing combinations, instead of one or two punches, is much more unpredictable and can confuse your opponent. This is especially true when you change up your combinations. When you get your opponent in the right position, unload on them with a heavy number of punches. Look at what Mike Tyson did to Marvis Frazier, and you will know what I'm talking about. I went over several types of combinations in the first book.

High Work Rate

A bad sign for a pressure fighter is when a boxer is landing a higher volume of punches than them. A great example of this is during the last couple of rounds in the first Mike Tyson and Evander Holyfield fight. Holyfield was known as more of a boxer and counterpuncher; however, he was blasting his aggressive opponent with nonstop punches, and Tyson was able to do little about it. Eventually, the referee had to step in and stop the fight.

This type of situation usually occurs later in the fight when the pressure fighter is losing gas, and the boxer still has a full gas tank. If you ever find yourself here, it basically means you didn't ante up enough. Not only do you need to improve your skills, but you also need to increase your work rate. Boxers will rest during moments when a fighter eases up. Do not allow them to rest. Keep up the pressure, so they always need to react to something. This will wear out your opponent and allow you to swarm them with little to no resistance.

A Good Jab

No matter what style you have, a good jab punch is essential for your repertoire. Going in headfirst with power punches leaves you open to a counter. It is much harder to not telegraph a power punch because of the extra body mechanics that are involved. Therefore, a pressure fighter who only relies on power punches will get destroyed. A jab offers a quick strike from almost any angle that can stun your opponent, or at least distract them, leaving them wide open for a barrage of punches.

Along with steadily stalking your opponent, a good jab will help you close the distance. Never ignore your jab, even if you are a pressure fighter.

Proper Defense

As a pressure fighter, as you inch closer to your opponent, you must be able to avoid getting hit. Otherwise, you will be pushed right back to the starting point or get knocked out. The bottom line is, being a pressure fighter is not just about overwhelming your opponent by throwing a massive number of punches. You must also have a great defense.

Pressure fighters are open to counterpunches. If it comes from a hard puncher, it can get you into a lot of trouble. When you are on your way in towards an opponent, slip, duck, bob, weave, keep your guard up, your chin tucked, and whatever defensive maneuvers you need to do to avoid getting hit. Once you are in range, you can unload with your punches, but don't get careless. Continue to practice good defensive tactics.

Take a Punch Well

It is impossible to avoid every single punch that is thrown at you. Punches are going to land, whether on the chin, on top of the head, on the body, or somewhere on the periphery. If you cannot take a punch, you will be in a world of trouble, no matter what style you employ. There are certainly defensive tactics you can employ to avoid getting hit, but they will not be effective 100% of the time.

Lennox Lewis is a great example of a pugilist who has a softer chin but good defense. Both of Lewis' professional losses came as the result of one punch against Oliver McCall and Hasim Rahman. At the same time, Lewis has shown to be able to take punches too, which was apparent against opponents like Ray Mercer and Vitali Klitschko, who are both heavy hitters.

As a fighter, you will have to learn how to take punches better, especially if you plan to start sparring and/or competing. I will go over some drills to help you with this later on.

Counterpuncher

Counterpunching is a skill that takes an immense amount of time to master. The boxing world has produced many great practitioners of this style, including Floyd Mayweather, Sugar Ray Robinson, Muhammad Ali, James Toney, and Bernard Hopkins. While this fighting style does not win over fans like a pressure fighter would, they might be some of the most skilled practitioners in the sport and produced some of the greatest legends. Many experts consider the names I mentioned above to be in the top ten list for the greatest boxers of all time.

To employ this style, you must have a great boxing mind, extreme patience, good reflexes, a strong sense of timing, and the ability to set traps by thinking several moves ahead of your opponent. Fighters with good distance and range are usually meant for this style of fighting. The essence of becoming a counterpuncher is that you know how to use your opponent's style and patterns against them. Often times, this involves studying their tendencies mid-fight and getting an idea of how they operate. When you watch a great counterpuncher in the ring, it is like seeing a magic act because they will literally stand in front of their opponents and not get hit. It is quite a sight to see.

So, what is a counter punch? It is simply a strike landed by a boxer directly following an attack by their opponent. A counterpuncher can also throw a punch while their opponent is loading up a shot. Basically, it can be a preemptive strike. The emphasis of counterpunching is more on defense than offense.

Counterpunchers are very cerebral in their approach, almost like a chess master. By reading a fighter's style and movement, they can time their shots at the perfect moment. Usually, this is when the opponent is fully committed or overextended. Basically, they will strike when they see the biggest openings.

There are several ways that a counterpuncher can capitalize on someone's mistake. The following are some of the most common:

- When an opponent is loading up a heavy shot, the counterpuncher can throw a faster punch before the other fighter gets their momentum.

- When your opponent overextends after throwing a punch and is fully exposed, they are vulnerable for a perfect counter.
- When an opponent is resetting after a jab, a good counterpuncher can slip a jab and then catch their opponent while on the way out.

Getting Opponents to Commit

A counterpuncher can be thought of as a salesperson who is trying to con them. Basically, they are trying to sell something that is not there. What this means is they are causing their opponents to commit to a punch by thinking they can land, only to find that there is nothing to hit.

A good counterpuncher knows how to make his opponents react. Once they do, then the counter-reaction will come. For example, jumping in and out of range, tapping with a jab, moving side-to-side, and circling the ring are all great techniques to get your opponent to commit. The key is not to let them know what you are doing because you are setting a trap. You will have to set many traps throughout the fight and constantly think on your feet.

Eventually, your opponent will catch on if you are always setting the same trap. This means you have to do something different all the time to keep your opponent guessing. For example, after an opponent has thrown a couple of right crosses and received a counter strike, they will learn to stop throwing that punch. The counterpuncher will need to entice his or her opponent into throwing something else.

Combining Offense and Defense

Counterpunchers are masters at being defensive and offensive at the same time. When they are slipping, ducking, blocking, or parrying, they could also be striking. Remember that you can't be predictable, and you need to land enough punches to at least win a decision. Defensive tactics do look great during a fight, but what determines a winner ultimately is the number of strikes that actually land. This means you have to create enough openings to land good solid punches. Otherwise, your opponents will win, especially if they were the aggressor.

Slugger

The sluggers are usually the biggest power punchers in boxing. They are often heavy-handed individuals who will hurt you no matter what type of punch they throw and whatever angle it comes from. Famous practitioners of this style were George Foreman, Sonny Liston, and Vitali Klitschko. They are known for barreling down on their opponents and landing big bombs. Often times, one or two punches is all it takes. This was evident when George Foreman fought Michael Moorer in the 1990s. Moorer was winning hands down on points until the massive power puncher landed his bombs and knocked Moorer out in the tenth round. This made Foreman the oldest heavyweight champion of all time.

The slugger's style is exciting to watch but does not look very scientific, especially compared to a counterpuncher. However, it is not easy to become this type of fighter. A lot of focus needs to go into developing devastating power. You will also need to build a body that is solid and have the proper mechanics to release all of your power all at once. When you hit someone, it should feel like they were hit by your whole body.

A slugger can also be known as a brawler. They need to have raw strength and the ability to take a hit. It is not elegant or technical, but it is highly effective when done properly. Unlike the pressure fighters, sluggers do not look to overwhelm their opponents by using a flurry of punches. They rely heavily on brute force, toughness, a strong chin, and natural punching power. The goal is to knock an opponent out as quickly as possible.

Sluggers are not known for immaculate footwork and don't move around the ring very much. If you want to be a slugger, you need to put in a lot of work on the heavy bag, trying to improve your ability to deliver dangerous blows. Sluggers are the dream opponents for counterpunchers because they often have to commit to their punches fully to get the powerful impact they need. This is why sluggers need to be able to take a lot of punishment too. Their defensive skills will not be on par with other fighting styles.

This fighting style favors a certain body type. Generally, it is those who are solidly built, either because of their genes or because of an effective strength-building routine. Sluggers want to see their opponents on the canvas, not being able to get up. Basically, if you want to be a slugger, focus on the following aspects:

- Build up your raw power by lifting weights, hitting the heavy bag, and whatever else you need to do to become stronger.
- Focus on creating a body type that can sustain punishment. A lot of your opponents will be looking to wear you down with body shots.
- Create a stronger chin, or at least learn to keep it tucked in.

- Work on your cardio because you may need a large gas tank to keep going before you are able to find your mark.

A slugger will be vulnerable to many different tactical strategies, so if you plan to engage in this fighting style, focus hard on your strengths and make them as effective as possible.

The perfect opponent for a slugger is probably a pressure fighter. This is because they need to get into close range to be effective, which brings them right into range against a slugger who can throw massive bombs. A perfect example of this was Joe Frazier against George Foreman. Frazier was absolutely decimated by the larger, stronger Foreman when they were both in their primes.

Boxer-Puncher

The boxer-puncher is a hybrid style of fighting with some of the technical skills of a counterpuncher and the punching ability of a slugger or pressure fighter. This might be the most effective strategy to employ because it gives you the best of all worlds. This style is difficult to master, though, and requires dedicated training to every aspect of boxing. This is why so many professionals do not go down this route. I doubt you can be average on all fronts. You truly have to develop expertise in every area. A person who masters this style will have many tools in their arsenal.

Against a slugger, a boxer-puncher can stay out of range and work on counterattacks. Against a pressure fighter, they can still throw damaging attacks on the inside, which will throw them off their game and hurt them, as well. Pressure fighters often hate getting pushback from other pressure fighters. Against a counterpuncher, they can skillfully get on the inside and do some damage.

A good boxer-puncher can change up their strategy multiple times during a fight. For example, they can act like a counterpuncher early on to wear down their opponents and then switch to a puncher's style to inflict damage when their opponents become tired.

To choose this style, you need to have some long-range to attack your opponent from a distance. In addition, you must be somewhat muscular to employ real power when you punch. One of the best examples of this style might be Roy Jones, Jr., who was incredibly skilled during his prime. During the 1990s, Jones could masterfully counterattack his opponent and also had some tremendous punching power. He was able to knock down, or out, multiple opponents throughout his career.

If you want to become a boxer-puncher, you will have to put in the training time. This may be the closest thing to a perfect fighter there is. However, they can still be beaten. Remember that a good boxer-puncher will not be as powerful as the greatest sluggers and certainly not as technical as the greatest counterpunchers. A great practitioner of any of these styles can lure a boxer-puncher into their type of fight and then beat them in this manner.

These are some of the most well-known boxing styles out there, and depending on your strengths and weaknesses, determine what works best for you. A major focus needs to be on your body style, as well. If you are shorter and stockier like Mike Tyson, the pressure fighter's style may be something to look at. If you are taller and lankier, then being a counterpuncher might be right up your alley.

Developing a Chin

I mentioned the idea of being able to take a punch earlier. This is true, no matter what style you engage in. While some people are born with a better chin than others, there are certain exercises you can do to strengthen that chin. Also, continue working on improving your defense to make your chin harder to find. The following are some strategies you can start employing today, so those punches from your opponent are less likely to take you out.

Build Up a Strong Foundation

One of the reasons fighters get hurt more than they should is because of poor conditioning. This is especially true with the legs, which give you support, stability, and balance. Therefore, focus on increasing the strength and endurance of your legs. Remember that when you are boxing, you are not just using your upper extremities. You are fighting with your whole body.

When you get hit by a solid punch, your legs become like jelly, making it harder to stand and support yourself. You will also be less mobile, so your opponent can swarm in and land more punches. The more durable your legs are, the quicker you can recover. Squats, lunges, leg presses, and leg curls are all great exercises to introduce into your training.

Strengthen Your Neck

When you receive a major impact anywhere above the neck, your brain can be jolted in multiple directions and suddenly crash on the inside of your skull. This can result in a knockdown or knockout. The jaw area is especially critical because any force here will cause your head to move in a certain direction while muscles and bones act as stoppers.

As a fighter, you never want your neck to snap back or rotate quickly because this will cause more volatile movements of your brain. By building up your neck muscles, you will develop natural shock absorbers. This will minimize the possibility of massive neck movements. The following are a few exercises you can use to strengthen your neck muscles:

- Dumbbell Shrugs: Hold a dumbbell in each hand. They don't have to be too heavy. Stand straight up with your hands at your side and your palms facing inward. From here, pull up your shoulders in a shrugging motion, hold for about one second, and then bring them back down. You can do about ten reps.

- Single-Arm Dumbbell Row: Find a comfortable workout bench. Stand with your right knee on the bench and your left foot flat on the floor. Bend forward but keep your back straight. Keep your right hand on the bench for support, and use your left hand to lift up the dumbbell by bending at the elbow until your elbow is above your body. Do about ten reps and then switch sides. Don't use too heavy of a weight to avoid straining.
- Lateral Raises: Stand straight with your feet shoulder-width apart. Have a dumbbell in each arm with your palms facing inward on each side of you. From here, lift both arms simultaneously until they are sticking out perpendicularly to you – your body will look like a capital "T". Your arms should form a straight

line when up. Hold this pose for about one second, and then bring your arms back down. Do about ten reps.

- Front Dumbbell Raise: With this exercise, stand similar to the lateral raise, but keep your hands in front of you with your palms facing towards you. From here, lift one of your arms straight up until they are slightly more than parallel to the floor. Hold the position for about one second and then bring the arm down. Repeat on the other side. Only move your arm and not your body. Perform about ten reps.

For all these exercises, perform about three sets. For a good visual representation of these and other exercises, check out the Video Tutorial section on the Basic Boxing Bundle – you will find a link to a video to help with neck exercises.

Watch Opponents Carefully

The punches that often finish off a fighter are the ones they do not see coming. Therefore, never let your guard down because a punch can come out of nowhere at any time. Even if it's not a particularly hard punch, it can catch you by surprise and put your lights out. If you anticipate the punch, you will be able to brace for it, and it won't do as much damage.

Do Not Collide

A punch will have more impact if you collide with it. For example, overcommitting a punch will cause you to move forward, making you vulnerable to a devastating counterpunch. Therefore, keep your body square as much as possible, even when you are throwing punches. Pull back on your punches quickly, so you are not left wide open for a long time.

Increase Conditioning

The better conditioned you are, the more punishment you can absorb. Physical conditioning needs to be a top priority, especially when it comes to endurance. When you get hit hard, your brain sends multiple signals throughout your body, causing your muscles to react in certain ways. How well you recover depends on how much stress your muscles can tolerate under these circumstances.

Conditioning includes your workouts, diet, and other aspects of your lifestyle. You must learn to build up lean muscle, reduce weight, and not decrease your strength. I will go over conditioning and diet in more detail in further chapters.

Take a Beating

Get used to getting hit by going to the gym and letting people pound on you. It is never fun to get hit, but it is something you must get used to. The more often you take a beating in the gym, the more likely you will be able to take it during competition.

We are just hitting the tip of the iceberg here. The remainder of this book will go into more detail about various aspects of the boxing game.

Chapter 2: #2 How to Get Seriously Fit for Boxing

In a boxing match, you never know how long a fight is going to go. It could be over within a couple of minutes or go the distance. Boxing another person for just one round is exhausting. Now, imagine doing it for several rounds. If you do not have the stamina and endurance, you will be taken out of the fight at some point. This is why it's important to get seriously fit if you want to become a boxer.

Boxing and conditioning are heavily linked to one another. If you are not well-conditioned, it will be exceedingly difficult to survive within the sport in the long run. Fatigue is debilitating and can make cowards out of all of us. No matter how skilled or tough you are, if you have an empty gas tank, those qualities become moot.

Imagine pitting a Corvette against a Honda Civic. Both of them are great cars, but if you were to put them against each other in a race, the Corvette would blow the Honda out of the water. However, if the gas tank of the Corvette is empty, it is not going anywhere, and the Honda will win despite have a less impressive engine.

Before you even enter a boxing gym, you need to have a base level of conditioning. Otherwise, you will be left behind during various circuits and training when you decide to enter a boxing gym. You might be surprised to learn that a large portion of training that boxers do occurs outside of the ring. These routines will be a major focus in this chapter. If you try to enter a boxing gym and perform all the circuit training, it is similar to jumping into the deep end of a pool when you don't know how to swim. Learn some basic swimming skills first before jumping into the deep end. The goal is to challenge yourself without taking unnecessary risks.

Good conditioning will not only improve your stamina and fighting ability but also help prevent injuries. Cardiovascular and resistance training will strengthen your muscles, tendons, and ligaments, getting them more used to the shock that happens with impact.

What to Know Before Your First Boxing Workout

Boxing is a popular workout amongst the fitness community, even for people who never plan to compete. The various movements, drills, techniques, and training exercises will target every area of your body. The following are some of the items you need to know before engaging in your first boxing workout.

- Show up with an open mind and be prepared for anything. Come in early so you can perform the proper prep work, like wrapping your hands and stretching.
- Do not expect to be perfect on your first day. Even if you are a fitness expert, your first boxing workout will be different from anything you are used to.
- A lot of equipment is not required. For your first workout, all you will need to do is show up. There are many exercises that can be done by just standing in one small space.
- Wear clothing that allows for good mobility. Tight-fitting shirts, or tank tops, shorts, and comfortable shoes are

essential. If you can get boxing or wrestling shoes, that will be perfect.

- If you are using boxing solely for fitness, do not be afraid because the bags don't hit back.
- Be mentally prepared to give it everything you have. Having this mindset will make you feel much better in the end than being timid or anxious.
- You will feel sore but also empowered. A good boxing workout is great for the soul because you will feel like you put the work in.
- Always remember to have fun. You will get more out of your workout this way.

Increase Your Stamina and Strength

As I mentioned before, much of the training that boxers do happens outside of the boxing ring and even the gym. To be a successful boxer, you will have to improve your stamina and strength at the same time. The focus of this section will be to go over various exercises that will build up these attributes.

When you exercise regularly, your body will learn to utilize oxygen more efficiently for your muscles. Over time, this will vastly increase your endurance levels, and you will feel less tired after training sessions. From here, you can keep upping the ante. Also, when you focus on certain exercises geared towards strength, you will be able to handle greater loads for a longer period of time without feeling fatigued.

Stair Climbs

Stair climbs are a great way to increase your stamina. An easy way to do this is to take the stairs instead of elevators every time you have to go up a few stories. When you climb up the stairs, do not do it gingerly. Put a pep in your step and move quickly but safely.

You can also include stair climbs into your workout routine. This can be done using real stairs or a stair master. On your first day, do it for as long as you can. I don't expect you to kill yourself here, but you should definitely feel the burn. Use this as your baseline, and keep increasing your time and intensity as you go on.

Cycling

Cycling, whether riding a real bike or a stationary bike, is another way to build stamina and work the various muscles in your legs. It is also a low impact exercise and a great alternative to running.

Side Planks

Side planks are great for strengthening your lower and side abdominal muscles. This will help you absorb vicious body blows from your opponents. To perform these, lie down on your side. Using your elbow for support, lift up your entire body at a downward angle towards your feet. From here, hold this position for at least 10 seconds. Increase your time daily and perform on each side. Below shows the Side plank using the elbow for support.

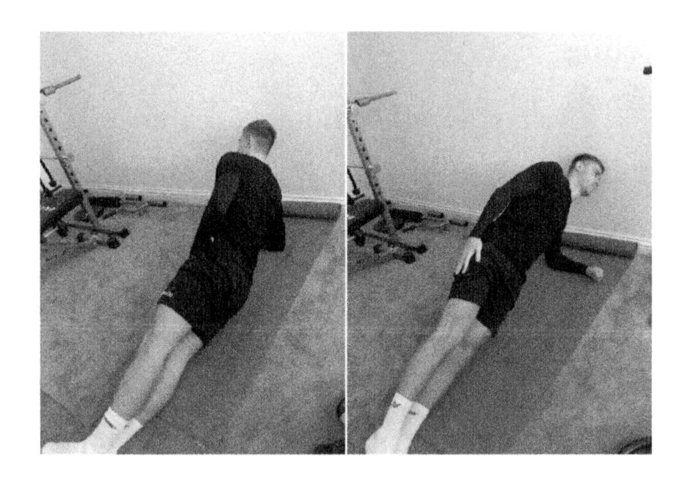

Push-Ups

Push-ups will strengthen your upper body and core muscles tremendously. They will target many locations on your body, including your biceps, triceps, chest, shoulders, back, and even legs. To perform these, lie down on your stomach with your palms facing the floor near your chest. Push-up slowly while putting all your weight on your palms. Once you are up, hold this position for a few seconds before going back down. Repeat at least ten times and increase your repetitions day by day. Remember to always bend at the elbows. To work out a greater variety of muscles, you can position your hands at different widths to perform different sets of push-ups.

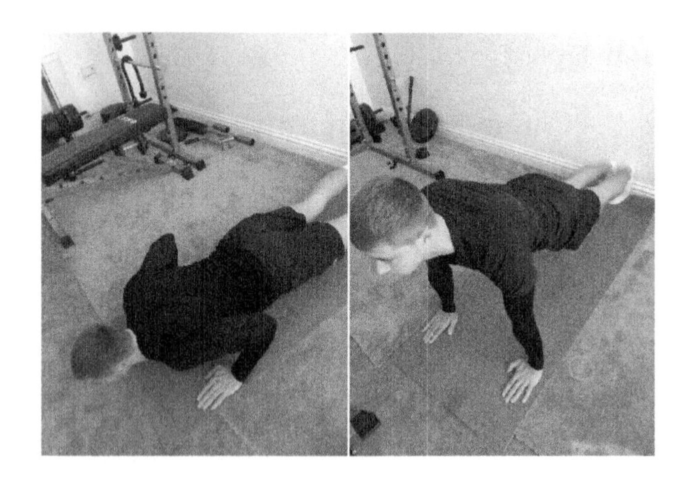

Dips

Dips are great for working out your shoulders, back, biceps, and triceps. If you have two bars slightly wider than your shoulders that you can fit between, this will be perfect. Grab onto the bars and push yourself up. Hold the top position for five seconds and slowly go up and down while bending at the elbows. Another option is to use a bench. Stand in front of the bench and place your arms behind you to support yourself. Bend at the hips and keep your back straight, similar to a sitting position. Bend at the elbows while going down and hold this position for about five seconds before pushing yourself back up. Repeat about ten times, increasing the repetitions each day.

Squats

Squats target many different muscles. In fact, they can work out your entire body while strengthening your tissues and ligaments. To perform a proper squat, stand with your legs slightly more than shoulder length apart. Keep your back straight and your knees slightly bent. Bend down at the knees while pushing your hips slightly back. Avoid putting stress on your back, so keep it relaxed and straight the whole time. As you become more comfortable, you can add weight to build more strength.

Mountain Climbers

Mountain climbers will target your quads, deltoids, biceps, triceps, obliques, hamstrings, and abdominal muscles. You will feel your heart pumping faster with this full-body workout. Your first step is to lie face down on the floor. Lift up your body by supporting it on your hands and toes, like a push-up position. Your alignment should be kept straight. From here, pull one of your knees towards your midsection and hold the position for about five seconds. Put the knee back and then repeat with the opposite side. Perform about five repetitions on each side and increase the amount daily.

Wall Sits

This is a simple exercise that looks just like it sounds. Get into a sitting position with your back against the wall and your arms locked at the elbows. Keep your back straight and your knees at a 90-degree angle. Your hamstrings should be perfectly parallel to the floor. Basically, you are sitting against a wall without a chair. Hold this pose for at least ten seconds and repeat four more times. If you are comfortable with ten seconds, increase your time with each rep. You should feel some burning over your thighs.

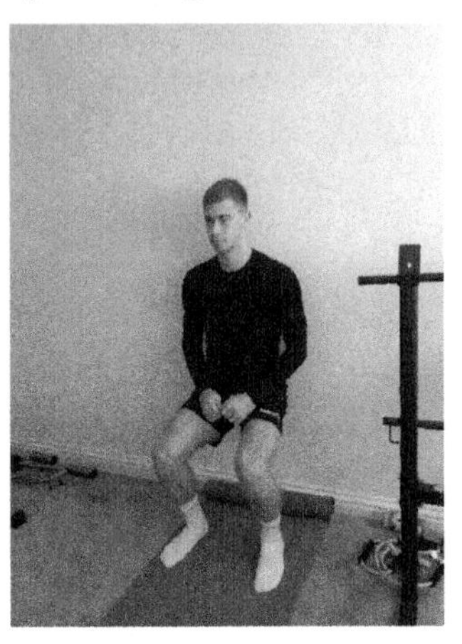

Lunges

Simple lunges are a great exercise for your back, legs, hips, hamstrings, abs, quads, and glutes. To begin, stand with your feet shoulder-width apart and keep your back straight. Step forward with your right leg while bending your hips, so both knees create a 90-degree angle. Your back knee should remain slightly off the ground, and your front knee should not go past the ankle. Hold the pose for five to ten seconds and then stand back up. Repeat for a total of five repetitions and increase the amount as you go along. When you feel comfortable, you can add weights to help increase your strength.

Running

Running is a great form of cardiovascular exercise that builds up your conditioning and stamina. While you are running, you are using your arms, legs, and various core muscles. Once again, it is a full-body workout that helps you lose unnecessary weight and build lean tissue. The impact you make on your legs while running will also help build up your bones and muscles. This is the main advantage it has over other aerobic workouts like cycling, swimming, or using the elliptical, which are also great. Run for five minutes on your first day and then increase your time and speed as the days go by. You will be surprised at the amazing shape you get into when you run. Plus, you can do it on a treadmill, around a track, on the road, or in the woods.

All these workouts I mentioned can literally be done anywhere, and you don't need the gym or equipment. A combination of these exercises will help build up your stamina and strength while targeting every area of your body, so you will be ready to enter that boxing gym with some confidence.

Strengthening Your Midsection

I spoke in chapter one about how to improve your chin and ability to take shots to the head and face. However, many of the punches you take will be towards the midsection. These shots are vicious, and if they land in the right spot, they can take a fighter right out of commission. Bernard Hopkins took Oscar De La Hoya out in their match with one brutal punch to the liver. Trust me, those strikes hurt.

You need to get ready for these types of blows because they will be common for many fighters, especially pressure fighters who utilize them regularly to break down their opponents. Surprise your opponent's when you get into the ring by barely being fazed from a body shot. Let's go over some ways to increase your body blow taking capacity.

Block and Parry

The best way to be ready for body shots is to avoid them completely. This means you have to improve your defensive skills, which I discussed in the first book and will detail further in a later chapter. You will need good hand-eye coordination since this is essential because you need to anticipate a punch being thrown at you.

Extending the elbows to cover the midsection partially or fully from punches is a common strategy employed by boxers. This is why it's important to keep your arms close to you. Also, you can dip left to right to help provide further coverage. Finally, you can use the parry to deflect punches completely and set yourself up to deliver a good counter. To perform an effective parry, you must use your opponent's momentum against them. You are basically deflecting their punch away from you. You can use your front or rear hand to deflect the shots your opponent throws at you, whether you parry their punches down, up, or to the side.

With a parry, you are not chasing a punch. Instead, you are letting it come to you and then moving it out of the way. Therefore, do not let your hands get too far away from your face or body; otherwise, you leave yourself too vulnerable.

Improve Your Explosive Shell

The explosive shell is the sliver of time your body and muscles use to tighten up right before the moment of impact. Basically, you are bracing yourself for an accident. Improving your explosive shell will improve your body's resistance to taking shots.

A common way to train your body to receive damage is by laying on the ground and having someone drop a medicine ball onto your abdominals from a certain height. You can also have someone lightly hit you with the medicine ball on all sides of your abdomen while you are standing up and flexing. Right before the medicine ball hits, you must exhale to tighten your abdominal muscles right before impact. Start with a light medicine ball and increase the weight as your shell strength increases.

You can use other objects besides a medicine ball; however, this is generally the most common and safest practice. Legendary boxer, Manny Pacquiao, uses a bamboo stick to hit his midsection while he's doing crunches. Other fighters will often have their training partners hit their abdominals with pads or actually throw punches to that area.

Perform Core Exercises

In order to condition your midsection, you must target your core muscles, which include your abdomen, pelvic muscles, rectus abdominis, erector spinae, and obliques. Needless to say, they cover a wide area of your body and are responsible for a lot of our movement and strength. Stomach crunches are a great start, and you should do them often as a boxer. The stronger your core, the more stable you will be. Other exercises that increase core strength are:

- Planks.
- Side planks.

- Leg raises.
- Flutter kicks.

Perform these routines on a regular basis, and you will feel your abdominal muscles strengthening up in no time. More core exercises with descriptions can be found in my Circuit Training Series – you will find boxing training and circuit training to go really well together.

Take Shots to the Midsection

One of the most effective ways to strengthen the midsection is to take body shots during sparring sessions. This will get you used to getting hit in the area. Sparring provides a real-world simulation of what an actual boxing match feels like, just in a controlled environment. Have your training partner focus on hitting you primarily with body shots so you will get used to taking them and defending against them. Letting the body shots land is also a good indicator of your strength around the midsection.

Learn to inhale and exhale quickly while flexing your abdominal muscles and core at the same time. The objective here is to try and bounce your opponent's punches off clenched abdominal muscles. Once you engage your explosive shell, it prevents punches from penetrating your body. If they do, you will be in a world of pain.

The Pugilist's Diet

If you listen to some of the top boxers throughout history, you will learn about how disciplined they were, not just with their training but also with what they eat. A boxer who has sustained a long career did so because they paid close attention to their diet. Boxers have to stay fit and maintain weight in between fights. Otherwise, they will have major fluctuations in weight, which is neither healthy nor beneficial towards their career. Most professional fighters hire a nutrition expert to make sure they are eating the right foods that are healthy and provide the essential nutrients their body needs. I will go over some components of a healthy diet for a boxer.

Carbohydrates

Carbs are needed to maintain a sufficient energy supply. The right carbs will release energy slowly throughout the day, replenish your depleted glycogen levels, and improve stamina for workouts and competition. Carbs are essential for many metabolic processes, and they should not be avoided in a healthy diet plan, despite what the fitness world tries to tell you. The important thing is that your intake of carbs is done responsibly and intelligently.

We need to make a distinction between simple carbs and complex carbs. Simple carbs have a high glycemic index and create significant fluctuations in blood sugar levels. They flood the body with excessive amounts of sugar, giving us a high. The influx of sugar causes our bodies to release insulin to help regulate everything. The insulin release leads to feelings of tiredness, which is commonly referred to as a "food coma." When you are in this state, the last thing you want to do is train or compete. You would much rather take a nap. Simple carbs are considered the "bad" carbs and include things like:

- Pastries and cakes
- Frosting
- Plain sugar

- White bread
- Anything with a white/wheat flour base

Complex carbs are considered the “good’ carbs because of their low glycemic index. They do not have an immediate effect on blood sugar or insulin levels. Complex carbs take longer to absorb, which is why they provide energy for a longer period of time. These types of carbs are much better for a fighter to take and include things like:

- Beans and lentils
- Sweet potatoes
- Wholegrain bread
- Oats and honey
- Fruits and vegetables

Complex carbs will generally lead to fewer health problems down the line than simple carbs.

Proteins

Proteins are essential for the construction and care of muscles. In order to train and compete properly, and also perform activities of daily living, we need to care for our muscles. Boxing will put a lot of wear and tear on your muscles, especially when you are sparring or competing. Proper protein intake can serve to prevent long-term muscle damage by helping to regenerate cells and tissues while also improving muscle mass.

Most nutritionists recommend about 35% of your daily nutritional intake comes in the form of proteins. Some of the best forms of protein include:

- Chicken
- Fish

- Lean meats
- Eggs
- Shrimp
- Greek yogurt
- Cottage Cheese
- Peanut or almond butter
- Beans

You can also take supplements like whey protein. When preparing meats, avoid frying or breading so you can achieve the best results.

Fats

Fats have gotten a bad reputation over the years, but they are essential to many body functions. That being said, not all fats are created equal, and boxers must focus on the "good" fats. Fats play a major role in cell building, energy maintenance, and the absorption of vitamins and minerals.

Good fats are usually the unsaturated kind. Other fats, like Omega-3 and Omega-6, are not created by our bodies and essential to take. These essential fats are important for brain function and can be obtained through diet and supplements. Boxers need to take in fat in order to perform at their optimal levels. Some of the best sources for "good" fats include:

- Olives and olive oil
- Avocado and avocado oil
- Seafood
- Walnuts
- Flax seeds
- Fish oil
- Coconut oil

Avoid fats like butter, corn oil, or vegetable oil. Even with "good" fats, you need to eat them in moderation.

Water

I cannot emphasize enough how important water and hydration are for a boxer, or anyone, in general. It is crucial to overall health, weight loss, energy, performance levels, and so much more. The recommended amount is 2 liters a day, but this can vary based on activity and training levels. Drink water throughout the day and also carry a bottle of water with you. If you find yourself getting thirsty often, it may be time to increase your water intake.

Also, avoid taking anything that will reduce your fluid levels, like soda, caffeine, or alcohol. These substances have a diuretic effect and can reduce hydration levels in your body. If you must have these products, at least take them in moderation.

Bernard Hopkin's Diet

Bernard Hopkins is one of the most successful boxers of all time and the oldest world champion in history. His career spanned multiple decades, and even well into his 40s, he was beating top-level competition that was often more than ten or 15 years his junior. Hopkins is extremely disciplined about his training and diet regimen, which has allowed him to stay healthy and relatively injury-free throughout the years.

Hopkins loves to follow a strict diet plan. He has actually referred to soda as "liquid crack," and his cheat meal is a peanut butter and jelly sandwich. He is a proponent of cooking his own meals because restaurants often do not have what he wants. He is careful about his nutrition and avoids fast food at all costs.

When Hopkins is training, he mostly sticks to fish, lean chicken, various plant proteins, fresh vegetables, and a lot of water. He occasionally eats red meats, but rarely. He avoids any foods that are high in sugar and sticks to wholesome ingredients that make him feel good. He listens to what his body tells him. He does not drink any alcohol. Being from Philadelphia, one would think Hopkins is a fan of Philly cheesesteaks. However, he avoids this kind of food. He mostly sticks to organic and fresh food from the farmers' market.

Floyd Mayweather's Diet

Floyd Mayweather is another all-time great, and one of the reasons for his long-term success is the disciplined approach he has towards his diet. Mayweather sticks to organic foods and avoids junk, like excess sugar or saturated fat. Of course, he has been known to like a twizzler or two. Here is a rundown or Mayweather's typical day:

- Breakfast: Eggs, grits, and home fries. He also loves turkey sausage. On the morning of a fight, he will likely stick to something light, like a banana and a glass of water. He also enjoys a good cup of coffee.
- During the day, he also drinks fresh fruit and vegetable juices made from organic foods.
- He loves to drink coconut water as it provides hydration and electrolytes between workouts.
- Lunch: He typically enjoys fish, like salmon or tilapia. He does not eat pork.
- He is a big fan of spaghetti.

- Dinner: Later in the day, his meals can include many things, like oxtail, mashed potatoes with gravy, and broccoli.

Mayweather has his own chef and has been known to call him at all hours of the night or day if he is craving something. He certainly has his cheat meals like fried hot dogs and anything with barbecue sauce.

When you start training as a boxer, you must focus on your physical training, but also what foods you ingest. Do your research and even get guidance from a professional. Many gyms provide service for a low fee. There is no one-size-fits-all diet plan out there, and you really have to assess your own body and metabolism to determine what is right for you. Just remember that food should never make you feel awful.

Chapter 3: #3 Practise Advanced Techniques for Successful Boxing

Now, we are getting to the good stuff. In the previous chapter, more of the focus was on general conditioning on how to improve strength and stamina. The focus of this chapter will be geared towards various boxing workouts and drills that you can do at home. To a certain degree, you can improve your boxing skills without having to step foot in a gym. I covered many basic exercises in the first book and will not describe them again here.

Advanced Punching Techniques

Just as a reminder, I described many basic punches in part one, including:

- Jab
- Cross (Head and body)
- Hook
- Uppercut
- Overhand

Many professional pugilists stick to these basic punches; however, many also rely on more advanced punch types. I will describe some of them here.

Corkscrew Punch

The corkscrew punch is thrown while twisting the shoulder, elbow, and wrist in one swift motion. At the completion of the punch, your thumb should be facing down and palm facing outward. Many fighters avoid this punch because it feels awkward, but when executed properly, it can have many advantages:

- Hand protection is a major benefit. Many boxers injure their thumb with power punches. With a corkscrew punch, you can ensure that your knuckles come into contact with your opponent first, and your thumb remains protected.
- Throwing a corkscrew punch will leave your chin less vulnerable towards a counterattack. As you throw the strike, your shoulder will naturally come up and cover your chin. Try it out yourself and see how your natural body mechanics work.
- It leads to a better defensive posture. As you throw the corkscrew punch, you are forced to lean at a certain angle that makes it harder for your opponent to catch you with a counterpunch.

The corkscrew punch should be dedicated more to power punches and not so much for jabs. The reason is that it reduces the speed, and a jab is meant to be a quick strike. Furthermore, body mechanics and angles make it more difficult to follow up with meaningful punches. The uppercut is also not recommended for the corkscrew technique because it is just awkward. The following are some of the best punches that work well with a corkscrew method:

- Corkscrew cross: This is the easiest punch to throw using the corkscrew maneuver. This power punch will hit your target quicker than any other power punch.

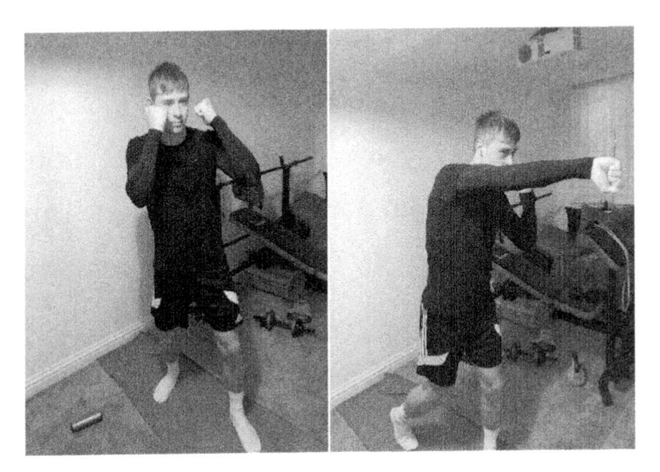

- Corkscrew lead hook: The lead hook is an effective punch, but it leads to many thumb injuries. If you find yourself prone to hurting your hand with hooks, throwing it with a corkscrew motion can significantly cut down on these injuries. A lead hook is thrown from the front arm when you are in your boxing stance.

- Corkscrew rear hook: The rear hook is thrown from the back, and it can be difficult to reach your opponent and make an impact with your knuckles. This is especially true if your opponent is at an awkward angle. With the corkscrew maneuver, you can hit your target more easily without damaging your wrist. This is because you will have more forearm support. No photos included as the final position looks exactly like a normal hook from the angle the photo was taken at – watch videos that I linked in the bundle instead to avoid confusion.

- Corkscrew overhand: This is similar to a rear hook but comes from an above angle. An opponent will have a much more difficult time blocking or moving away from this punch. If you are copying the form of the pictures below, make sure you don't spend too long in the position of photo 2 – I included that to show you how you should raise your elbow to the side to get the overhead angle.

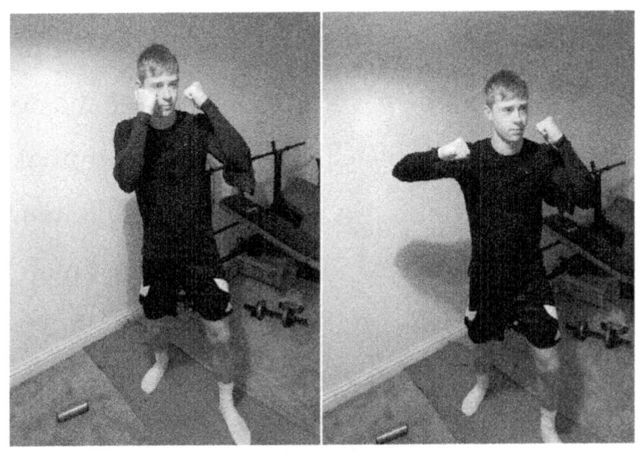

Leaping Lead Hook

The leaping lead hook sounds simple when you describe it, but it is difficult to master and execute. It is just like a regular lead hook, but you are jumping in towards your opponent at the same time, which will create a greater impact. Before you can master this punch, you have to look at all of the elements involved, including:

- Body positioning
- Movement
- Timing
- Accuracy
- Technique

When you perform this punch incorrectly, you are leaving yourself vulnerable to a major counterpunch that you are essentially leaping into. Here are some ways to effectively throw a leaping lead hook:

- Measure your distance: Never lunge at your opponent from too far away, or it is a dead giveaway. Your opponent will see you coming from a mile away. This punch should only be attempted when you are a few inches outside of range.
- Jump height: When you are jumping, you should not be trying to slam dunk a basketball. Your feet should only leave the mat by an inch or two. The best technique is to never really leave the canvas and move forward in more of a gliding motion.
- Bend at the knees: Your knees should always be slightly bent from the moment you leap to when you land. Bending at the knees creates a more stable frame and

allows for quicker escape in case you miss.

- Keep it short: This refers to the angle of your hook. Do not come in too wide because it will reduce your speed and power.
- Control your power: This may sound confusing, but too much power can be a bad thing. This will cause you to follow through with your hook instead of pulling back, which can lead to missing wildly and getting off balance. You will also be open to heavy counterattacks.
- Keep up your guard: Always keep your chin covered and your rear guard held high.

This is a very risky punch that you should not try until you have some experience and increase your fitness level. If you miss, it can create a lot of problems for you. Roy Jones, Jr.

and Floyd Mayweather, Jr. are two legends with effective lead hooks. The photos below show the starting position right before you leap forwards and the position you should twist into to land the hook – this is hard to demonstrate using photos so remember the videos are in the Basic Boxing Bundle.

Multiple Lead Hooks

There are a few fighters out there who can throw multiple lead hooks in a succession of three, four, or even more. Once again, this is a high-risk attempt, and you need to make sure you follow the proper technique. The following are some tips to throw successful multiple lead hooks.

- Throw quickly: Whenever you throw multiple punches of the same kind in a series, the key to pulling it off is quickness.
- Throw short: When throwing punches in a series of three or four, you must be in close range so you can keep the punches short. If you need to extend, you are going to be slow and make yourself vulnerable to a counter.
- Target the head: When throwing multiple punches in this manner, the power will not be as great since the focus is more on speed. Therefore, you should aim for the head when throwing multiple lead hooks because these weaker punches will have

little effect on the body. In the end, it will probably wear you out more.

- Control your power: Every punch except for the last one in the series should be thrown with more speed and less power. Only the last punch should have significant power behind it.

Throwing fast lead hooks will cause your opponent to cover up, which allows you to throw a final power punch. You need very quick hands and fast-twitch muscles to pull this technique off. Yet again, the photos below only show two left hooks but hopefully that shows you how quickly each hook should be thrown and your arm shouldn't be brought back that much between each punch as it should be quick.

Double-Cross

The double-cross is more effective and less risky than multiple lead hooks. To throw a successful double-cross, you will need to follow these steps:

- Throw a regular cross but do not follow through on it. The objective is to throw your opponent off by blinding their vision temporarily.
- After hitting your target, pull your arm back a few inches.

- Extend your arm again to hit your target one more time.

The double-cross should also be done quickly. These punches are great for stunning your opponent and setting up other power punches and body shots.

Advanced Punching Combinations for the Heavy Bag

The heavy bag is one of the most useful tools in a boxer's arsenal. It is a great way to improve strength and physical fitness. The heavy bag must also be used to increase and maintain skills by practicing a wide range of combinations. Many simple combinations can be used, like a jab-cross or jab-hook. I went over several of these simple techniques in the first book, so the focus here will be more advanced combinations. Please be sure to practice these combos to a point where it feels natural.

Straight Right-Left Uppercut-Right Hook-Left Hook

After sticking out your right hand, get inside and fire the left uppercut. This can immediately be followed by a right hook and a left hook.

Right Uppercut-Left Hook to the Body-Left Hook to the Head

This can be a highly effective combination with great timing and one that you should practice regularly on the heavy bag. The right uppercut at close range can be helpful penetrate your opponent's guard, or at least cause their guard to rise. From here, you can land a nice left hook to the body. The fighter will instinctively drop their guard, leaving them open for another left hook to the head.

Left Hook-Left Uppercut-Left Hook

This whole combination is done with the same hand, which makes it more challenging to pull off. The left hook will temporarily stun a fighter, and the uppercut can penetrate the guard, which leaves an opening for another hook.

Left Hook-Right Hook-Left Uppercut-Right Hook-Jab

When you are close, the left hook can enter from an outside angle and does not need to be fully committed. The right hook and left uppercut that follow are where the power will lie. The hooks and uppercuts come from different angles, which can throw a person off completely. The combination will do a lot of damage. The ending jab is used to keep your opponent preoccupied while you step out of range.

Jab-Right Upper Cut-Left Body Hook-Left Head Hook

The quick jab will be used to distract an opponent, and this will pave the way for a straight right hand, followed by a right uppercut. Throwing the uppercut from the same side as the straight right will make it even harder for an opponent to defend against. The final punch is the left hook, the power of which comes from the front foot, assuming that you have an orthodox stance.

There are a variety of different smart combinations you can come up with. If you want to watch someone who was masterful at these advanced combinations, check out some of Juan Manuel Marquez's fights.

Shadowboxing

Shadowboxing is a training method that has been used by practitioners of boxing since the sport first started. It is boxing without a physical opponent present and allows you to try out various techniques while punching through the air. Shadowboxing is also a great warm-up tool before hitting heavy bags or sparring. This training method is as much of a workout for the brain as it is for the body.

If you watch fighters shadow box, they look to be going through many different motions. It can even seem like there is no rhyme or reason to it. However, the fighters might be looking to practice multiple moves in quick succession. They are not just mindlessly throwing punches without any type of purpose. Well, at least the ones who are doing it the right way aren't. To make sure you get the most out of your shadow boxing session, I will go over some tips to help you become successful.

Emphasize Movement

Whenever you are shadowboxing, the emphasis of the practice should be on footwork and body movement. You should also be combining diagonal and lateral movement footwork with rolling. I advise you to shadow box in front of a mirror or even record yourself to observe your movement. Make the most of the space that you have.

Visualize an Opponent

Since you will not have a physical opponent in front of you when you shadowbox, you can still create an imaginary one. As you visualize this opponent, focus on various boxing techniques besides just landing punches, like cutting off the ring and performing different defensive strategies. Don't get sloppy just because there is no actual opponent in there. At some point, there will be, and you want to make sure you are as prepared as possible for that day.

Imagine your opponent as a dangerous person who is trying to take your head off. Also, picture yourself landing the right punches in the right spot. Turn this moment into a real boxing match.

Don't Allow Your Punches to go Through Your Target

As you fight your imaginary opponent, do not allow your shots to go through or past them. Try to land your punches right on the spot where your opponent is. If you are going through your opponent, it means you are overcommitting on your punches, and this is a bad habit to get into. When you are fighting an opponent or hitting a heavy bag, your punch does not travel through the target. It stops upon impact, and the force generated travels into the solid object. Therefore, train for the situation of hitting the target.

Accelerate Your Shots

When shadowboxing with an imaginary opponent, picture snapping back their head as you accelerate your punches at the end, right before they reach their target. This will help you improve your punching speed and power.

Use Weights

To help increase your hand speed, you can always add some light weights of one or two pounds and use them while you shadowbox.

This may not seem like much, but you will notice how much easier it is to throw punches once the weights are gone, especially as more time passes. Try shadow boxing with weight for a round and then shadow box without them. You will notice a significant difference in your hand speed.

Have Themes for Your Rounds

As you shadow box, you will split it into rounds. For example, you can do five, three-minute rounds. Incorporate a theme for each round. You can picture yourself with a pressure fighter for the first round, and for the second round, picture yourself against a counterpuncher. Use these visualizations to practice what you would do against these varying opponents.

Watch Others

Watch other boxers, whether you train with them or watch them on TV. Study all of their movements, down to the last detail. For example, assess how they move their feet and legs when they punch. Incorporate the actions of these successful boxers into your shadowboxing routine.

Benefits of Shadowboxing

Shadowboxing is a training method used by many pugilists in the boxing world, and for good reasons. Even the best in the sport, like Muhammad Ali, used this training technique in their routine. First of all, it is a great warm-up, so engaging in this practice can slowly increase the heart rate and get you loosened up before hitting the heavy bag or sparring. Shadowboxing will produce a lot of growth for you in the ring and will make you a contender at any level. The art of shadowboxing should never be discarded. Let's go over some more benefits of this routine. A link to a video on shadowboxing is included in the bundle, so it will be very helpful to learn from.

Form

While shadowboxing, you can truly pay attention to footwork, punching technique, head movement, and other strategies without worrying about getting hit back or injuring your hand on a heavy bag. There's no pressure to throw fast punches or anything of that nature, so you can use this time to build better fighting habits. Your stance is a significant area of your style where you can focus on, especially:

- Keeping your feet in an ideal position with proper weight distribution.

- Bending your knees slightly for improved balance and stability.
- Making sure your feet remain diagonal and slightly wider than shoulder-width.
- Keeping your elbows down and hands up for proper defense.
- Looking forward while keeping your chin tucked towards your chest. This helps your chin from getting exposed.

Movement and Balance

When you first start boxing, do not be surprised if you start tripping over your feet more often or losing balance. You are not moving in a manner you are used to, and getting the proper form can take a while. Movement and balance are important factors in having success in the ring. This becomes even more difficult when someone is coming at you with a barrage of punches.

Therefore, shadowboxing is a great time to focus on these skills. As you shadowbox in the ring, really pay attention to your footwork and how you move. Throw in some sidesteps and pivots while you are at it. As your movement becomes more fluid and your balance improves, you will notice yourself improving during your heavy bag and sparring sessions.

Improved Muscles Memory

When you improve your muscle memory, you will be able to perform complex tasks and movements while on autopilot. Basically, the various techniques will become instinctual, and you won't have to think about them. With shadowboxing, you will be repeating many of the same movements over and over again, and they will slowly become second nature. Having muscle memory is crucial to being a boxer, where you will have to make many defensive and offensive movements quickly and effortlessly.

The great thing about shadowboxing is that you will be in complete control of your surroundings. This will give you the opportunity to focus on specific techniques, including punches, head movement, and moving your feet. If you use a mirror or film yourself, you will be able to watch your mistakes and improve them, as well, before they become a habit.

Mindfulness

Shadowboxing helps with mindfulness, which is having the ability to be aware of your surroundings, thoughts, and actions. You will be fully present in the moment. As you shadowbox regularly, you will develop more ring presence. Mindfulness allows you to become calmer and more focused. If you watch closely, it will become apparent that the greatest boxers have control over their emotions in the ring, even when things are not going well. You will need to develop this demeanor as you grow as a boxer.

Before getting on the bags, mitts, or sparring in the rings, perform some shadowboxing techniques. No matter how advanced you become in boxing, never stop doing this type of training. You can include this in your cardio exercises if you choose.

The Stance Switch

You may remember from the first book where I discussed orthodox and southpaw stances. The orthodox method is used primarily by right-handed fighters, while left-handers use the southpaw method. Most fighters are comfortable in their familiar stance; however, I will discuss the stance switch in this section. This is when you will be able to switch from orthodox to southpaw, and vice versa. This can confuse your opponent and set up angles to throw some more powerful bombs, like hooks and uppercuts.

Great care needs to be taken before you perform a stance switch. I will go over some general rules for performing an effective stance switch that will help put you in a perfect position to do some damage to your opponent:

- You need to be in close range to your opponent, or at least, at mid-range. The whole idea is to be up close and personal, so you are close enough to land some big hooks and uppercuts. Mike Tyson was a perfect example of a fighter who knew how to unleash some fury on his opponent after performing a stance switch.

- It needs to surprise your opponent and cannot be predictable. Therefore, do it after some sort of trigger, like throwing a punch or performing a feint.
- Once you become advanced in your skills, you can use the stance switch at long range if your opponent is coming towards you. You can switch at just the right time as your opponent moves forward and catch them with some brutal shots. Do not attempt at long range if your opponent is standing in one spot or moving away. They will see it coming if you do.

Orthodox to Southpaw

I will start by explaining the orthodox stance to the southpaw stance. With the orthodox, you will have your left foot in front.

- From your back foot, initiate by explosively pushing from the ball of the foot and bringing it forward.
- As you are pushing, take your front leg and pull it back. Your upper body will follow the movement.
- You will end up in a southpaw stance and be at a right-angle to your opponent.
- Remember that you have to become very quick and fluid in your movement and perform the steps simultaneously.

Of course, if you are in a southpaw stance and want to switch to orthodox, you would use the same movement but with the opposite legs.

Orthodox to Orthodox

You can also perform a stance switch but remain at the same stance. Here is an orthodox to orthodox stance switch.

- Initiate by taking the front foot and explosively driving off the ball of the foot, pushing it towards the rear.
- Simultaneously, take your back leg and pull it forward. Your upper body will follow the movement.
- You will end up at a right-angle towards your opponent and remain in an orthodox stance. From here, you can unleash some hooks and uppercuts.

You can practice the stance switch often while you are shadowboxing.

Some Things to Consider

As with any other boxing techniques, some common mistakes need to be avoided. Avoid these faults during your drills, so you are less likely to make them during sparring or competition.

- Avoid leaping off the mat. The stance switch needs to be a quick motion to move from one position to another.
- Keep your guard up during the whole switch; otherwise, you will be vulnerable to an attack. Do not loosen your guard, either. Keep it solid the entire time.
- Be explosive in your movement, so nobody can see it coming.
- Perform the stance switch with the intention of throwing a shot or two. If not, it is just a wasted movement.

Throwing lead hooks and uppercuts from the front side is useful when performing a stance switch.

Shifts of Attack

Many individuals will watch boxers on TV and notice that they shift away from their opponents in various directions. To the untrained eye, this can look like a fighter is exiting from the fight and trying not to engage. However, the fighters are getting out of range and creating opportunities for different methods of attack. I will go over some movements that boxers can make in the ring to help them get into better positions to attack while not getting hit. When you practice, whether it's shadowboxing, heavy bag work, or sparring, try employing all of these strategies so you are not one-dimensional in your movement.

As you perform these shifts of attack, it is important to maintain a good stance and defense. Never forget about the basics when it comes to more advanced techniques. The following are some significant shifts of attack to put yourself in a better position to throw punches:

- Straight-line: This is a simple maneuver where you simply move straight back. Push off your front foot and move your rear foot first.
- Lateral shift: First, with your lead leg, make a quick movement laterally, followed by your rear leg. It may be better to throw a strike with your back leg before moving the leg laterally, followed by the front leg. After moving laterally in the lead leg's direction, you can always do some kind of pivot to put yourself into a better position.

- Diagonal shift: Move at a 45-Degree angle in the direction of your back leg, moving the back leg first and pushing off the front.
- Retreat to attack: With this movement, you can move back in various directions, so there is a more significant opening for an attack.
- Pivot and straight line: Pivot on the lead leg, moving the back leg in either direction. From here, move back in a straight line.
- The pass: With this technique, you will be moving closer to your opponent's strong arm if they use the same stance as you. Therefore, it's better to perform this after a punch is thrown with the rear arm. Roll under the punch and then move diagonally in the direction of the lead foot.

Various Drills

Power, speed, and footwork, etc., are some of the crucial aspects of boxing that you must work on. Even if you are not a power puncher, your punches should still be able to do some damage. While you don't have to be Speedy Gonzales, you must be quick enough to move out of the way and hit your target before they have a chance to move. I will go over some various drills that you can employ almost anywhere to improve your boxing skills. Some equipment may be involved with specific exercises.

Medicine Ball Throw

Almost any boxing gym you go to will have medicine balls of various sizes. Medicine ball throws will train your arms to be more explosive, and you will be able to generate more power through your muscle fibers. Here are some common exercises to try:

- Lie flat on your back and hold a medicine ball in front of you. Using both arms and your chest, throw the ball up as high as possible and then catch it with both arms.
- While standing in your boxing stance, throw a medicine ball by pushing it off the palm of one of your hands. The movement should be similar to throwing a punch. You can either throw the medicine ball against a wall or have a partner catch it.
- Stand with your feet a little greater than shoulder-width apart and bend slightly at the knees. Hold the medicine ball at center abdomen with both hands. Throw it aggressively at a trampoline that is slanted so the ball can bounce back to

you. Catch it with both hands as it comes back.

Plyometric Push-Ups

Plyometric push-ups can aid in power and speed by training your arms, shoulders, and pectoral muscles. To perform these properly:

- Get into a standard push-up position. Go down as usual, but as you rise, explode back up so that your hands lift off the ground.
- Keep your core muscles tight throughout the whole process.
- If you are able, you can quickly clap your hands together in mid-air as you explode off the ground.

Work the Heavy Bag

The heavy bag is the most obvious way to increase punch power. You will feel a lot of resistance, especially as you increase the solidity of the bag. Of course, just standing there, throwing lazy punches will not do much for you. Be explosive with your punches and perform intervals of successive punches for about 10-15 seconds. After each interval, keep moving your feet and upper body before going for another 10-15 seconds.

Perform these routines for about three minutes, with a 30-60 second break in between rounds.

Squats with a Medicine Ball

A large portion of your punching power comes from your legs. You can perform squats using a medicine ball to create a more substantial base eventually.

Use a Speed Bag

Using a speed bag can improve the timing and quickness of your punches. Take small swings at the bag while switching hands continuously. This routine will help your fast-twitch muscle fibers in the upper back and shoulders.

Use Hand Weights

As you shadowbox, you can start adding weights to your hands to create more resistance. Your goal should be to match the quickness of empty hands as you increase the amount of weight. When you throw punches without these weights, you will notice a significant increase in punch speed and output. The weights do not have to be heavy. Two or three-pound weights are plenty.

Jumping Rope

While performing jump ropes, pump your knees up and down while moving your wrists swiftly. You can perform jump ropes quickly for about 30 seconds and then slow down for 10 seconds. Jump rope sprints like these are a great way to develop the muscles needed for fast punches.

Box Jumps

Box jumps give boxers more spring in their steps, which improves their footwork. Box jump exercises are fairly simple. You can stack one or more boxes in front of you and then jump with both feet on top of them. The key is to jump with explosiveness each time. Perform as many repetitions as you can and increase the amount each time. Also, do not start with too much height on the boxes, or you can get severely injured.

Step Drag

This drill helps fighters make sure they keep their feet on the ground. Focus on moving just a few inches at a time. To start, get into a boxing stance, step with one foot in any direction, and reset the other foot to get back into the original stance. Make sure to reach with your toes of the stepping foot and push off with your toes of the dragging foot. You can be quick with this routine, but you don't have to be explosive. Remember not to take broad steps and do not jump or lift your feet. This technique allows for quicker and less predictable movement.

Small Pivots

Perform small pivots where you swing your back leg clockwise and counterclockwise. Make sure to stand relaxed and only turn about 15-Degrees at a time. Make these pivots slow and calm, so you are focusing on technique. You can mix these in with step drags as you become more comfortable. Also, you can start practicing the various punches that you have learned.

I hope you enjoyed all of the various drills and techniques in this chapter. There is still plenty more to come.

Chapter 4: #4 Training 1-on-1 for Excellent Fighting Experience

Imagine being a tennis player and hitting the ball against a brick wall. You can work on several techniques like this and improve your mobility, reflexes, and hand-eye coordination. However, at some point, you will reach a plateau. There is only so much training you can receive by hitting a tennis ball against a brick wall. At some point, you need an opponent to hit the ball back to you at different angles to get more practice. Also, hiring a coach can help you understand your strengths and weaknesses.

This same concept holds true for boxing, as well. In the previous chapter, I went over drills that you can perform on your own. If you feel that solo training is enough based on your goals, that's okay. However, if you want to advance, you will need some one-on-one training. This is one of the most effective ways to improve your boxing abilities. You will receive the personal attention that is geared to your needs using some customized programs. This exercise program will create maximum results for you that are exponentially greater than being in a group class. A personal boxing trainer will also focus on strengths and weaknesses and help you use those to your advantage.

One-on-one training will also be very motivating. You will have 100% of the trainer's attention. They will have a vested interest in helping you reach your goals. Also, they can provide you with a lot of positive energy. Unfortunately, with group classes, you can become lost in the shuffle.

When you have reached this moment in your training, I highly advise you to take a personal trainer route. You will be able to set up your schedule and see them as much or little as you would like. While personal sessions are more expensive, you can still find reasonable deals on sites like lessons.com and thumbtack.com. Many trainers also offer private sessions online. There are many options out there for you, and I hope you will continue to improve upon your boxing skills.

One more thing to note is that your personal boxing trainer can provide you with more routines and techniques for you to practice at home. For the remainder of the chapter, I will go over many different one-on-one training methods and how they are beneficial.

Focus Mitt Drills

If you have ever watched highlight reels of boxers training for competition, you have probably seen many clips of them practicing on focus mitts. The trainer will hold up mitts on both hands for the boxer to punch from different angles. The various drills allow a fighter to practice a varying level of punches, good head, and body movement, footwork, and defense, while also getting a great workout and increasing their stamina.

You can certainly get creative with your focus mitt drills, but you should still follow some guidelines to get the most benefit out of this training. It is time to go over some useful exercises.

Jab Call-Out

This is the most basic drill out there. The fighter and trainer simply move around the ring and pop off jabs. It's a great drill for newcomers to help them practice the most basic punch in the sport. It is also a great warm-up routine and a way for them to increase strength in their weaker arm that is used to throw a jab.

Here are Some of the Routines for a Verbal Call-Out

- As the fighter and trainer move around the ring, the trainer will call out "jab" and flash the mitt. The fighter will hit the mitt with a jab. The trainer may also call out "double jab."
- Call out "jab to the body." The trainer will hold the mitt lower and allow the fighter to practice a body jab.
- Call out "jab to the head and body."

The Other Method is Known as an Auto Response

- The trainer does not say anything. They will just flash the mitt, and the fighter will hit it as soon as possible.
- The next step is to show the mitt but take it away quickly. This way, the fighter will learn to respond faster.
- Next, you can show one mitt, and after they hit it, show the other mitt so that they can hit that one too.

Here is the Method for Defense then Counter

- The trainer will call out a defense maneuver and then give an opportunity for a jab. So, then the trainer says, "slip then," perform a slip and then jab towards the mitt.

- The trainer can also throw a punch at the fighter without calling out a defensive maneuver.
- Finally, the trainer can throw a punch at the fighter without calling it out and immediately flash the mitt for an opportunity to counter-jab.

Putting Everything Together

- The trainer can call out a jab, throw a counter at the fighter after they punch, and then flash the mitt to give another counter-jab opportunity.
- The trainer can call out a jab, give another jab opportunity by showing the mitt, and end by throwing a counter to test the fighter's defensive skills.

- The trainer can call out a jab; once the fighter throws the punch, step to the side, and flash the mitts again.

Combination Punching Drills

The important part of this drill is to remain steady and relaxed at all times. When calling out combinations of punches, it is easier to label the punches as numbers to make it easier. Here is the key:

- Jab=1
- Right cross=2
- Left hook=3
- Right hook=4
- Left uppercut=5
- Right uppercut=6
- Body shot=b

Based on this key, you can come up with various punch combinations. For example:

- 1-1: Double jab
- 1-3-4: Jab-left hook-right uppercut
- 1-b-4-3: Jab-body shot-right hook-left hook

You and your trainer can come up with several punching drills and don't even have to start with the jab all the time. I hope that you appreciate the variety.

Defense and Counterpunching

This focus mitt drill is used to train auto-defense and countering. This is a real boxing skill because you will have to be able to defend and counter at the same time. Many fighters become overly focused on offense that their defensive skills are almost non-existent. When they do practice defense, it feels unnatural. On the other hand, some fighters become excessively focused on defense and lack punching power and effectiveness.

The drills in this section will help you learn where to look during a fight. Many beginners have a hard time seeing what is coming their way, and these exercises can improve their insight.

Blocking Defense Drills

With these routines, the fighter is only blocking.

- The fighter and trainer will move around each other while the trainer throws out single jabs. The fighter will simply block.
- The fighter and trainer will move around each other, and the trainer will throw random looping shots at any moment.
- The trainer can throw some jabs towards the head and body.

- The trainer will throw combinations of multiple punches.
- The fighter and trainer will circle the ring, and the trainer can jump in at any time to throw a flurry of punches.
- The trainer can move around, near and far, and open up with any random punches he or she wants.

Remember, as the fighter, your goal is to block during these drills and not merely throw counter attacks.

Blocking and Counter Drills

With these drills, you can start combining your blocks with counterpunches.

- The trainer will call out a jab and then immediately throw a jab back after the fighter hits the mitt. The trainer can even throw a jab at the same time the fighter is throwing one.

- Call out a 1-1-2 combo, and then the trainer will throw a counter jab once the fighter is done. Refer to the key above for the punch types.
- The trainer will call out a 1-2-3 and throw a 1-2-1-2 combo after the fighter is done.
- The trainer will throw a 1-2-3-2 combo at the fighter and have them counter with a 2-3-2.
- The trainer will throw a 5b-6b at the fighter and make him block the punches while having them counter with a 5b-6b-3-2.

The fighter and trainer can come up with several different combinations to practice blocking and countering.

Slipping Defense Drills

The fighter will mostly be practicing slipping techniques here, and some blocking, as well:

- The trainer will throw double jabs, and the fighter can choose to block one and slip the other or simply slip both.
- The trainer will throw three jabs at the fighter, and they will try to slip all of them.
- The trainer will throw a 1-1-2 combo. The fighter can block the first punch and slip the next two.
- The trainer throws a 1-2-3 combo, and the fighter can block the first two and slip the last punch.
- In the final drill, the trainer can throw numerous straight punches while the fighter blocks all of them. Without warning, the trainer can throw a double-

hook, both of which the fighter rolls under.

Slipping and Countering Drills

- The trainer will call out a 1-2 combo and then counter with a jab. You will slip the jab.
- The trainer calls out a 1-2 and counters with a jab. The fighter will slip the jab and counter with a right hand.
- The trainer calls out a 1-2-3 combo, counters with a right hand, which the fighter slips and counters with their combo, like a 1-2 or a 3-2.
- The trainer calls out a 1-2-3-2 and then throws a double-hook. The fighter will roll under the hooks and counter with a 3-2.

Mitt work Drills for Improved Footwork

The critical thing with footwork is to remain relaxed and not move excessively. If you start jumping around and getting too excited, you are just wasting valuable energy. The objective here is to make your footwork as natural and effortless as possible. If you become overly anxious, you will start telegraphing all your movements, making it much easier for your opponent to see what is coming.

Pivot Drills

- The trainer will call out a pivot jab, and the fighter will respond by throwing a jab while pivoting their back foot. This will allow the fighter to throw a jab and then swing their body out of the way.
- The trainer will call out a 1-2-3-1p. The "p" means the fighter will pivot after the final jab, while the trainer will throw a

straight punch to see if the fighter can avoid it.

Fighting on the Ropes

- The fighter and trainer will stand close to each other as the trainer calls out various punches while also throwing punches to see if the fighter can pivot and avoid them.
- The trainer will lean against the fighter on the ropes. The fighter will have to pivot to create space, avoid strikes, and get off the ropes.
- Also, the fighter can be on the outside and practice keeping the trainer trapped along the ropes.

Various Movements

- The trainer will move backwards as the fighter pursues them while throwing punches on the mitt. The goal is to trap the trainer into a corner or against the ropes and not let them escape.
- The trainer will move toward the fighter while calling out various combinations. The fighter will hit the mitts while moving backward and try to avoid getting trapped on the ropes.
- The fighter can work on several combinations on the mitts and then move away to avoid getting hit back. The fighter can jump in again and throw more combos.

Style Drills

With the style drills, the trainer can mimic various opponents' styles and have the fighter respond with appropriate offensive and defensive techniques. Here are some examples:

- With a tall fighter, practice slipping jabs, rolling under long shots, closing the distance, and countering with body and head shots.
- With a short fighter, practice throwing quick combinations and then pivoting away to avoid significant blows.
- With a fast fighter, learn to defend against quick combinations and trick punches. Also, you can experience how to chase down a fighter who moves a lot and trap them.
- With a volume fighter, you can get used to fighting someone who is always coming at you with a barrage of punches. You can learn to defend against various attacks and set up your own counter strikes.

By all means, do not limit yourself to these drills only. They are just a starting point to give you an idea. When working with a trainer, both of you can develop a variety of drills to improve every aspect of your boxing skills. Take advantage of mitt work by practicing a wide variety of punches and defensive techniques.

Sparring

Cardio exercise is great for getting your heart rate up and getting fit. Shadowboxing is a great way to practice various techniques and movements, including punches, footwork, and body mechanics. Punching the heavy bag will allow you to feel what it's like to hit a solid object. Mitt work will let you feel what it's like to throw punches and work on various techniques while working with a trainer who is not stationary. Mitt work is considered the level before our final preparation phase, which is sparring.

Sparring is when you get into the ring against an opponent and fight. You will get a chance to practice and showcase all of the skills you have learned while getting strikes thrown right back at you. Before you ever decide to compete at any level, you will have to get into the ring and spar with somebody. There is no way around it because you need to understand what it feels like to get hit. It is one thing to practice your movements and create a strategy when you are shadowboxing or hitting the bag. However, when you get hit back, those strategies get tested in a significant way and might even have to be thrown out the window altogether. The more you spar, the more experience you achieve in this regard.

"Everyone has a plan 'till they get punched in the mouth."

-Mike Tyson

Tips on a Good Sparring Session

It can be very nerve-racking to get into the ring for the first time and spar with someone. If you have never been hit before, then trust me, it is not fun. However, it is a necessity if you want to enhance your skills further. Don't even think about competing at any level until you have done a significant amount of sparring.

One of the first things I recommend is that you spar with someone at your level or willing to be at your level. This means that if you spar against an experienced pugilist, they will not just come at you with a barrage of techniques and overwhelm you. This will not be immensely helpful unless your goal is to take a beating. I guess that's not a bad thing once in a while. However, the purpose of sparring is not to stand there and get beat up. You want to take these opportunities to work on your technique in a more pressure-filled environment.

Therefore, spar with someone at a similar skill level and close to your height, weight, and reach. As you improve your skills, you can slowly start getting into the ring with higher quality opponents who will challenge you further. I will go over some more helpful tips to make sure you get the most out of any sparring session:

- Start with a few sparring games where you and your opponent focus on specific techniques. For example, you can both agree just to throw jabs the whole session or have one person throw punches the entire time while the other fighter slips, blocks, parries, and uses various defensive tactics.

- Relax the power and focus more on technique. In a sparring session, both combatants will be hitting each other. However, the goal is not to take each other's heads off. Instead, use this opportunity to learn to fight in various situations.
- Try different combinations of punches while in a session. If both individuals in the ring follow the tip of relaxing the power, then you should have no fear of trying out new punch combos.
- If you don't know how hard to hit, gauge what your opponent is doing. Hit them as hard as they are hitting you. This will ensure that you are on par with whoever you are in the ring with. If your opponent is hitting you with softer punches and then suddenly wallops you with a power

punch, it could be a response to your own punches. Take a hint and ease up a little bit. Don't allow things to get out of hand.

- In some instances, you can remove the power altogether and just focus on speed and reflexes. Tip tapping may not be effective in a real fight, but it can train you in other ways, like agility, defense, punching technique, and various other components of the game. It's almost like two people shadowboxing each other.
- Keep a relaxed stance, but always make sure your hands are up, the chin is tucked, eyes are forward, elbows are in, and feet are in the proper position. Relaxing muscles will help prevent exhaustion from being overly tensed.
- Never drop your hands in a sparring session, even when you are tired. Even though you are not going full force, it

does not mean you cannot be knocked out with the right punch.

- Fight longer rounds with less rest. This will improve your cardio and teach you how to recover quickly. My suggestion is to spar for three minutes, with 30 second rests in between rounds. You can start with two minutes, with a one-minute rest, and then work your way up.
- Do not apologize for hitting someone. When people are not used to hitting others, they often apologize whenever they land a punch. Do not do this because it is aggravating. You are supposed to hit your opponent during a sparring session.
- When you get closer to the competition, you can start engaging in more challenging sparring sessions. This is when you bump up the intensity to about 90% or even 100%. Of course, make sure

to wear proper protective equipment, like gloves, headgear, and a mouthpiece.

- Don't make excuses for a lousy sparring session. Remember that it is your responsibility to show up and perform. Whether you are sick, hurt, exhausted, or anything else, if you are stepping into the ring to spar, you need to be ready. If you have a terrible performance, take responsibility for it, and make the proper corrections for next time.
- Don't show pain. When you are competing with someone, showing pain in the ring is like bleeding next to a shark. Your opponent will capitalize and go in for the kill. Practice not showing pain during sparring. Even when you get hurt, stay stoic.
- When sparring, focus on the body and head to get used to hitting both targets. Many times, newcomers are

headhunters. However, body shots can wear down your opponent and make the head harder to find. Many fights have even been won with well-placed body shots.

  - For real-life examples of vicious body shots winning fights, check out Roy Jones, Jr. vs. Virgil Hill, or Bernard Hopkins vs. Oscar De La Hoya.

- Always remember your manners. This is not a street fight or barroom brawl. You guys are competitors and need to show proper respect. Always touch gloves beforehand, acknowledge each other after the session, and never fight dirty.
- Practice circling away from the power. Always move in the opposite direction from your opponent's power hand.
- Always keep moving in some way in the ring. Remember always to make the

movement purposeful. You don't want just to be dancing around and wasting energy. Your goal is to avoid being a stationary target and put yourself in positions for good defense and offense.

The following are some tips for more advanced sparring sessions. This will be after you have gained some experience and are ready to start competing.

- Practice situational sparring. This is where you target situations that you don't feel comfortable in and have your opponent recreate them in the ring. For example, if you fight orthodox and have difficulty with southpaws, you should spar with a southpaw.
- Spar with people who are the most like your opponent. For example, if you are going against an opponent who is tall and

slim, spar with this type of individual. If your opponent is a forward-moving power-puncher, spar with a similar kind of individual.

- Don't get into the ring to just beat up on beginners. I don't want you to learn this information so you can become a bully, and I certainly don't want you to practice this in the ring. You will mess with the wrong person at some point, and you'll end up taking a whooping. Guess what? It will be 100% deserved.
- Use the experience you gain to help train others. When you teach someone else, you learn more yourself. Everyone wins in this regard.
- At some point, you need to focus on winning. When you first start sparring, it is okay to pay more attention to technique and not so much on winning a match. However, once you start

competing, your goal should be to win, and you must also have this mindset during sparring once you become more advanced.

Always remember that it takes time to become good. At first, you will be stumbling and making a lot of mistakes. That is okay because it is a learning experience from the beginning. The goal is to eliminate these mistakes and become more fluid in all of your movements.

Improving Reaction Time and Agility

Reaction time and agility are crucial aspects of boxing. You need to possess these skills if you want to have any level of success in the sport. All the training methods discussed in this book will improve all of these aspects of your fight game. In this section, I will go over some specific exercises to continue improving in all these areas.

Reaction Time

In the middle of competition, how quickly you are able to react can mean the difference between winning and losing. You never know when a surprise punch will be thrown your way, and you will never know when an unexpected opening will present itself. Being too slow in any of these situations can completely alter your result. Reaction time can also be known as a reflex, which is an action done related to a stimulus without conscious thought. For example, if an object is coming towards you, you will move out of the way without even thinking about it. I won't get into detail about the things I already discussed, like sparring or mitt work, but the following drills can help improve your natural and automatic movement for boxing:

- Use a double end bag, which is a moving target that will allow you to attack and defend at the same time. As you hit the bag, it will snap back towards you, and you must be able to retract your punch quickly and move out of the way in a swift motion.
- Use a punch paddle, which is similar to hitting a mitt. However, it's light and has a handle, so it puts less strain on the holder's back. As a result, they can carry it for much longer and move easily. This allows the fighter to throw punches from various angles.
- An elastic head ball is a bouncy ball attached to your gear with an elastic cord. This piece of equipment will allow you to throw straight punches in quick

succession as the ball's speed increases with each punch.

- There is also an exercise known as the coin catching drill, where you extend out your arm in front of you with your palm facing down. Next, place a coin on top of your hand. Throw the coin upward about 10 centimeters and try to catch it with the same hand. As you become better at this, you can add the number of coins being used.
- The next drill is the coin drop, which you will need a partner to perform. Stand about two arm’s length from your partner. Your partner will drop a coin from chest height, and your goal is to catch it with one hand.
- Foam sticks work similar to pads but are much lighter and allow for greater reach. This means you can punch from a wider

variety of angles and slip, block, duck, or parry more punches.

- With a tennis ball drill, you will stand against a wall in your boxing stance with your back heel touching the wall. Your partner will throw a tennis ball in your direction, and your goal will be to evade it. Your partner will throw the tennis balls at your head quickly and in succession, so you must be ready to react fast.

Perform these routines regularly, and you will see your reflexes and reaction times increasing effectively. Makes sure to increase the intensity and challenge as you go along.

Agility

When you are in a boxing ring, you will need to quickly and smoothly move in all directions. This is known as agility and is essential for continued success in the sport. You may have seen athletes in many different sports stop suddenly and then move in a completely different direction. This is because they have agility. For boxers, this translates to how good your footwork is. I will go over some drills you can start doing to improve your agility. As you work on these exercises, you will be able to move in any direction without taking your eyes off your opponent. You will even be able to confuse your opponent to a certain degree if you are quick and unpredictable enough. Let's get started with some drills:

- The side lunge: This is great for building strength in the outer muscles of the hip, glutes, and legs. Stand with your feet shoulder-width apart and take a large step towards the side with one foot and bend your knee while keeping the other one straight. Once you reach the bottom of your lunge, push back up quickly into your neutral position. Perform several reps on one side before switching to the other leg.

- Resistance band step slide: You will need a resistance band wrapped around both legs. Keep your feet slightly wider than shoulder-width and bend your knees to get into a low position. From here, take several side steps. Once you reach a wall or ending spot, reverse and move in the opposite direction.
- Lateral jumps: These drills improve your leg strength and help you quickly transition from one direction to another. All you have to do is draw a line on the floor or lay down some type of rope. Stand on one side of the line with both feet together and then jump back and

forth on both sides of the line quickly while keeping your feet together.

- Ladder sidestep: This exercise will significantly improve your speed as it relates to your feet. You will need to get an agility ladder. Lay it down with it extending out to your side. From here, step into the first box with your closest foot and then move your other foot right next to it. Perform this routine for the remainder of the squares. Once you have reached the end, go back in the opposite direction.
- Side-to-side shuffle: You will want a large area here. Place cones that are about 15 feet apart. Stand on the inside of one cone with your feet shoulder-width apart and bend down into a low squat position. Push off with the foot that is closer to the cone and take sidesteps towards the opposite cone. When you get to the other

cone, reverse directions. Increase your speed as tolerated.

- Mirror drill: This will require a partner. Stand facing your partner and make sure you are about five feet apart. From here, your partner will make various movements, whether they are footwork techniques, defensive maneuvers, or punches. Your goal is to copy them as closely as possible. Do these in five-second increments.

Agility in boxing works a little differently from football or basketball because the movements are different, and space is more limited. Therefore, work on agility techniques while working in a smaller area.

These various drills will also improve your balance and coordination, including hand-eye coordination. I will get into more drills in the next chapter that will enhance your performance in the ring.

If you speak to individuals who work out frequently, most of them will be happy to discuss their training routines with you. One of the concepts that will be consistent with each person is that they focus on workouts geared towards specific objectives each day. For example, they will focus on cardio one day and strength training the next. The same idea holds true for boxing drills. I recommend setting up a schedule to prepare for agility one day and combinations the next day. This type of program will make things less overwhelming for you so you can focus more on specific drills without getting too confused.

Chapter 5: #5 Further Boxing Tips and Tricks

I have already touched on the importance of sparring in this book. We will now focus on various techniques and strategies to make you a more dominant and sophisticated performer in the boxing ring. There is a lot to be aware of whenever you are sparring and competing. If you watch high-level professionals engage in certain movements, you can probably bet that they are doing it for a reason. They are not just a bunch of wasted movements. This chapter's focus will be to discuss specific drills that will make you a better ring general.

The Clinch

The clinch is a common boxing technique where a boxer ties up their opponent’s arms, rendering their attack useless. While clinching is technically illegal in traditional rules, many pugilists employ this tactic in the modern day. Most referees will allow a clinch for a certain amount of time and even let boxers to fight out of it independently. If a clinch is extended, the referee will usually break it up. If a fighter excessively uses this tactic, it can lead to warnings, point deductions, and even disqualifications. Many fighters used the clinch against Mike Tyson as he closed the distance to avoid getting hit by vicious combinations.

Many fighters will also use dirty boxing techniques by punching while in the clinch. These punches do not earn points on the judges' scorecards but do a considerable amount of damage over time. It is vital to learn and understand the clinch so you can use it to your advantage in certain situations. Of course, always be mindful of excessive clinching so you don't start getting penalized.

Use as a Strategic Maneuver

The clinch is mostly used as a strategic maneuver to tie up an opponent who is on the offensive. It is an effective way to nullify an attack, but make sure you are not taking an excessive amount of punches trying to perform this technique. If a fighter gets clinched often, it can wear them down physically and mentally. Practice using the clinch during sparring sessions so you can get an idea of how to use it in various situations.

Use to Disrupt an Opponent's Rhythm

Once an opponent finds their rhythm, it can be difficult to stop them. Clinching is a great way to disrupt their rhythm and throw off their momentum. Suddenly, they go from throwing a variety of combinations to becoming lost and confused. They will constantly have to reset, which brings them to a state of inactivity.

To execute a clinch properly, try it in various situations, so your opponent will never know when it's coming. You can employ this strategy, whether you are on the offensive or defensive. Eventually, your opponent's plan can become derailed entirely.

Neutralize an Opponent's Attack Preemptively

You can neutralize an opponent's offensive attack before it even begins. This will help you diffuse the situation and avoid having to deal with combinations. This strategy is useful against aggressive fighters who like to punch in massive volumes. Lennox Lewis, former heavyweight champion, was a master at employing this strategy.

To get into a clinch, you must grab your opponent's arms quickly and authoritatively. Otherwise, they will easily fight out of it and open up with a barrage of punches. Also, you need to make sure your opponent is in close range. You do not want to reach or strain to be able to tie up your opponent.

Conserving Energy

I have touched on the idea of saving energy while boxing because it is essential to complete, nevertheless, win a match. No matter how skilled, powerful, and quick you are, you're not going to last long if you run out of gas. You want to be fit before you ever step into a boxing ring for competition. However, you also need to reserve your energy while in the ring, so you don't run out of gas in the middle of a fight. Consider the following tactics:

- I already discussed clinching. You can use this time to catch your breath and lean on your opponent slightly to tire them out. This is especially true if your opponent is smaller than you.
- Do not perform meaningless movements. Your movements need to be unpredictable. Avoid jumping around, showboating, running, or doing anything else that does not serve a purpose. Don't throw punches just for the sake of throwing them. They need to be thrown with the intent of landing, closing the distance, or keeping your opponent preoccupied. If you are going to move, do it for a specific purpose.
- Sit down between rounds. Three minutes may not seem like a long time, but it is an

eternity in the boxing ring. This is why you need to take advantage of the rest periods between rounds and sit down on your stool.

- Make sure to take deep breaths. The funny thing is that when people become engaged, they often forget to breathe. However, taking deep breaths will allow adequate oxygen intake, which is necessary to keep moving.
- Don't forget to stay relaxed. So many people tense up during a fight, either because they think it's necessary or because they are nervous. You are wasting a lot of unnecessary energy by tensing up your muscles. Instead, learn to stay relaxed. Do not keep your fists clenched at all times. Keep your arms up but loose. Keep a strong base with a good stance, but do not tense up your leg muscles once again. It will take time to

relax in the ring, which is why you must spar frequently before you think about competing.

- Do not eat right before a fight because digestion burns a lot of energy. Eat at least a couple of hours before fighting and make sure the meal is not too heavy.
- Keep yourself hydrated. Ensure you are drinking adequate amounts of water throughout the day because your cells need it to function properly. Ration your water throughout the day. Do not drink to drink it all at once, right before a fight.

Use your energy wisely before and after a match. Once it is over, then you can go crazy and celebrate if you want.

Fighting with a Low Guard

Most boxing trainers, including myself, will praise the idea of keeping your guard high with your elbows tucked in. This is great for defense against headshots and body blows too. However, some fighters like to fight with their guard lower. While this is not the more common technique, it does provide some advantages, including:

- You can generate more power because you are throwing your hands from a lower position, which means you can engage your hips more and load up on your punches.
- It is excellent for blocking body shots. While you can block body blows with the more traditional high guard, your elbows alone are not as effective as using most of your arm.

- It is easier to slip punches because more weight is at center mass, which means there is less weight surrounding your head.
- It is good for fighters who like to fight at long range. They can thwart off incoming attacks.
- It can be confusing for opponents. Since many fighters do not fight with a low guard, doing so can confuse your opponent because they are not used to it. This is similar to an orthodox fighter going against a southpaw for the first time.

With the low guard, you will have to be very alert for punches that are coming your way. Especially those that are targeted towards your head. I would advise trying the low guard during your drills and not using it during competition until you are extremely comfortable with it.

Fighting in a Low Stance

For shorter fighters who are going against tall opponents, it can be beneficial to maintain a low stance. This can be done by bending the knees a little extra. Staying in a lower position can minimize the power from a taller fighter's punches. They will also have to exert extra effort and energy to connect punches on those who stay low. You can also generate more power from a lower stance.

Be careful, though, because maintaining a low stance can drain your energy if you are not careful. Therefore, make sure you train your legs so they are ready for this extra effort. Squats and calf raises are great for increasing endurance in the legs. Also, practice the low stance any time you shadowbox, spar, or work the mitts if you plan to make this part of your style.

Common Boxing Combinations to Try During Sparring

Sparring is a great way to practice combination punches against a real opponent. Many fighters get into the habit of throwing one or two punches at a time. However, you need to mix these up with longer combinations. Unless you are George Foreman, you probably will not take your opponent out with one punch. Also, one punch is much easier to block than a whole series of them. Therefore, you need to add several different combinations to your arsenal. The following are some of the most common punch combinations that boxers use:

- Jab-Cross
- Jab-Hook
- Jab-Jab-Cross
- Jab-Cross-Uppercut-Hook
- Jab-Cross-Hook

- Jab-Cross-Upper-Hook to the body-Hook to the head
- Right Cross-Left Hook-Right Cross
- Jab-Cross-Hook-Cross

Practice mixing these up during sparring sessions. While the jab is the most common lead punch to start a combination, you can lead with other types of punches when the moment is right. This will come with more experience and training. Once again, this is why it's essential to spar frequently if you plan on competing someday.

More Important Advice

Boxing is a tough game, and if you plan on succeeding long term in competition, you will need a lot of training and discipline. Finally, you will need to perform a lot of techniques in the ring and think quickly on your feet. I will end this chapter by going over some more essential advice you need to incorporate in your training:

- Enforce yourself on your opponent. This does not mean you have to be aggressive and stay on top of them. However, you need to make your presence felt. If you are just sitting back meekly, it won't be very effective in the ring. Your opponent will run all over you.
- Create many different angles for both offensive and defensive purposes. I covered many of these strategies with things like the stance shift and various shifts of attack. Remember that you are not just throwing punches for no reason. They need to serve a purpose. Therefore, create more openings by fighting from various angles.
- Learn to manipulate your opponent by making them do what you want. You will

need to learn many tricks that will cause your opponent to make a mistake or fall into a trap. From here, you can execute your plan of attack.

- Pace yourself for a long fight. You never really know how long a fight will last. It could go the distance. Even Mike Tyson, Earnie Shavers, and George Foreman did not knock out all of their opponents. Pace yourself in case the fight goes to a decision.
- Change the tempo on occasion. If you fight at the same level and speed the whole time, your opponent will get comfortable. Instead, turn up the intensity once in a while to keep your rival on their feet. Keep switching it up between slower punches and faster punches.
- Don't be hardheaded. No matter how much experience you have, you can

always learn something. Never act like you know everything; otherwise, you will stop growing as a boxer.

When you are ready, get into the ring and start sparring. Always wear the proper protective equipment, like hand wraps, gloves, mouthpiece, and headgear.

Chapter 6: #6 Winning the Mental Battle

"Champions aren't made in the gyms. Champions are made from something they have deep inside of them-a desire, a dream, a vision."

-Muhammad Ali

Over the months and years of training, you will develop some solid skills, endurance, strength. These will take you a long way in your boxing career. However, to join the ranks of the greats and reach that next level, having a healthy mindset is essential. When you are exhausted, in pain, and don't think you can go any further, the mindset you possess is what determines whether you keep going or not. In the end, mental toughness is what wins tough fights and helps you perform that last few minutes in the gym. If you train and/or compete in boxing long enough, you will get to that point where you have exhausted all of your resources, and the only thing that's left is your mind.

The mindset is just like a muscle in that it can be built up through various strategies and exercises. With the different techniques, I go over in this chapter, you will be more determined to win fights, improve your memory, have more concentration, and be more focused on your goals.

Experts in any sport will define mental toughness as having the psychological edge over an opponent. The good news here is that if you have decided to take up boxing, for whatever reason, you already have some mental toughness in you. Boxing is a challenging sport, and many people are not willing to engage in it. However, you still have a long way to go.

Training Your Brain

It is safe to say that boxing is a sport like no other and probably one of the most challenging activities to become a part of. In addition to physical strength and stamina, you will need to have laser-like focus and concentration, a lot of discipline and control, and the ability to think quickly on your feet. Remember that a fight moves very quickly and becomes very unpredictable. You may have to change things at the drop of a hat. The bottom line is that boxers have to be very mentally tough or never reach their full potential in the end.

Unfortunately, many boxers, even those at the professional level, do not pay enough attention to their mindset. They will often put it on the back burner, and when they are in a struggle, they have no reserves. Focusing on the other pillars of boxing, like technical ability, physical strength and endurance, and tactical awareness, can all lead to improved mental toughness. For example, when you become fatigued, you often become a coward. If you are well-prepared, you are more likely to have courage.

Developing a Fighter's Mindset

Fighters will often win fights, not because of their skill, but because they had the mindset to do so. Mike Tyson was notorious for intimidating his opponents to the point they were often paralyzed with fear. Of course, Tyson also had the skills to back up his intimidation. I am not saying that you can just think your way to victory. However, what ultimately separates the champions from everyone else is their mental toughness. In order to fight, you must develop a fighter's mindset. Here are some tips for developing the mindset of a champion:

1. You need to determine your "why" as in, "why are you doing what you do?" Your "why" needs to be something greater than just being good at what you're doing. There needs to be a deeper meaning here because you will always find someone better than you at something.
    a. For example, your "why" can be to take more ownership of your life. Whatever it is, it needs to be powerful enough to keep you going.
2. Stay focused on what you need to do. Avoid distractions because they will slow you down. When your mind is clear and focused, it will absorb things like a sponge.

3. Stay effective by tracking what you do every day. What did you accomplish? What were your victories? What were your losses? What do you need to change? Did you do what you said you would? What was your greatest struggle? Assess your day and decide how much progress you are making.
4. Become exceptionally good at what you do? Champions have confidence, but part of that comes from knowing how good their skills are. So, train hard and become the best you can be in the ring. There is no easy way out in this regard.

Practicing Mindfulness

People have a tendency to always be on the move and never stop, even for a moment. They believe this is the key to success. Even boxers believe that they have to train all the time in order to be successful. However, this is not true at all. As a fighter, if you are always training and overworking yourself, you will completely burn out your engine. Overtraining will not do you any benefits in the long run. Therefore, you need to find time to slow down and take in everything around you.

One of the most effective ways to do this is by practicing mindfulness. Mindfulness is the ability to become aware of your present moment. This is a great way to understand your emotions, thoughts, feelings, and physical sensations. Basically, it allows you to understand where you are and what you are currently doing. With mindfulness, you are living in the present moment rather than the past or future.

You may be wondering how this is helpful as a boxer. As I mentioned earlier, mindset has a lot to do with being mentally prepared, which is essential for success in the ring. Being mindful allows you to have a moment-by-moment awareness of everything that is going on. This means you can better understand what is going through your mind during a fight and remain more focused on your opponent. When you become mindful, you are often less stressed because you are not overthinking everything. Instead, you stay focused on what you are doing. As a boxer, you need to relax in the ring or waste excessive energy worrying.

Not only will mindfulness help you in competition, but also during training. You will be able to work out harder during your drills if you are present in your situation. Rather than worrying about what happened in your past or what might occur in the future, you will stay focused on your training.

Imagine being in the ring and not paying attention to your opponent, who wants to take your head off. Why are you not focused? Because you have troubles at home, you found out some bad news, you lost your job, or you just had a fight with a friend, etc. There are many reasons you can become distracted, but you never want to let these reasons enter your mind during a boxing match. Otherwise, you will be in a world of trouble. With mindfulness, this will not be a concern for you because anything outside of the present moment will not matter.

There are many strategies for mindfulness that I will go over. I recommend you incorporate some of these techniques into your training routine. Perform them throughout the day, including during your workout regimen.

Deep Breathing Exercises

Deep breathing will slow down your physiological processes and put you in a state of relaxation. When we are excited, our breathing is generally quicker, so purposefully slowing it down can combat our anxiety. To perform these breaths, stop what you are doing, inhale over a few seconds, and exhale over a few seconds. Use your abdomen and diaphragm while doing this. You will notice yourself slow down and have a clearer mind.

When you can, find a quiet place and sit down to perform this exercise. If that is not possible, you can take deep breaths while engaging in activities. I mentioned earlier that people forget to breathe while working out or competing. It is important to take deep breaths continuously for both energy conservation and mental clarity. Remember that you also have breaks in between rounds. You can use this time to perform deep breathing exercises, as well.

Mindfulness Shadowboxing

Shadowboxing is actually the perfect time to be mindful because it is necessary to focus on your techniques and movement. You can be alone in your space and be completely aware of your present moment. Use this time to pay attention to everything that's going on around you and within you. Every time you throw a punch, move your feet, perform a defensive maneuver, or anything else, be fully aware of what you're doing. You will learn a lot about yourself and your technique by doing this.

Body Scan

A body scan is when you stop and assess every portion of your body. You can start with the feet and slowly move up towards your head.

As you do so, take note of everything that your senses become aware of. Do not try to figure out what is wrong; just be observant of what you notice. Our bodies register everything that happens to us, so we can learn a lot about what's going on. For example, if we have aches and pains in our muscles, it can be due to overwork, growth, or mental anxiety.

Meditation

Meditation is a great way to relax, get rid of stress, become more focused, feel better connected to yourself, and reduce brain chatter. It can take years to become a meditation master. However, we do not need to become masters to take advantage of the many benefits. Meditation is a great practice to engage in every day, and the more you do it, the better you will become. From here, your fight game will only improve. The following are some steps that beginners can take to start incorporating this practice into their lives:

- Find a quiet area where you can sit comfortably.
- Choose a time line, like five or ten minutes.
- Notice your body's position, and make sure you can remain in this position comfortably for a while.
- Follow the sensations of your breath as you inhale and exhale.
- Recognize when your mind has wandered, which will happen on occasion. When you notice this, simply return your attention back to your breathing.
- Don’t obsess over your thoughts when your mind wanders. Just bring them back.

- Once you are done, notice how you feel and what is going on in the environment around you.

Meditation is a practice that can be done in the mornings, evenings, before engaging in any activities, or whenever you find time to do so. Meditation before and after workouts and competitions can be remarkably effective. There are numerous books out there dedicated to meditation, as well as many practitioners who have been doing it for years.

The truth is you can add mindfulness to almost any activity you are doing. For example, as you eat breakfast, you can slow down and take everything in. While taking a shower, you can do the same thing. As you walk to your car, you can stop and feel everything from your environment, like the air, the sun, or the smell of the flowers. The bottom line is that mindfulness can be employed at any time of the day.

Setting Goals

As a boxer, you will be accomplishing many feats, but if you want to get value out of your sessions, you need to set achievable goals, both short-term and long-term. This is true whether you plan on competing or not. If you don't set goals, you will not make any progress. This is not exclusive to boxing or fitness and extends into every area of our lives.

Boxing is a great way to learn how to set goals and accomplish them by specific deadlines. I will go over some simple steps to help you with this process.

- The first thing you need is to determine what your goals are. You need to be specific here and list what your daily, weekly, monthly, and annual goals are. For example, you can say that you will train for 30 minutes on the first day, increase it to 45 minutes by the end of the week, and reach one hour by the end of the month.

- Break the big picture down into smaller steps that are more achievable. If you want to start competing in six months, you can determine small milestones along the way. For instance, you can start shadowboxing and hitting the heavy bag by the end of month one. You can start hitting the mitts by the end of month three. You can start sparring by the end of month four. Finally, you can spar six rounds that are three minutes each, with 30-second breaks in between.
- Make sure to write your goals down somewhere and assess them regularly. I

would recommend weekly or at least monthly. Writing them down makes them more concrete.

- Take small steps each day that move you closer to your goal. If you want to work out on the heavy bag for 30 minutes by the end of week one, you can start with five minutes and then increase your time by five minutes each day.
- Adjust your goals periodically based on how you see fit. The chances are that your original goals will change along the way. Make sure you are aware of that and prepare accordingly.
- Your goals should be measurable so you can track your progress and also know when you have reached them.
- Make sure your goals are realistic. If you just started boxing today and plan to compete for the first time by the end of the week, that is not reasonable at all. Do

not try to kill yourself when creating deadlines.

- Do not compare your goals to anyone else because you are not them. Your timeline does not have to match others.
- Once you have reached your established goals, it's time to create new ones.

In the sport of boxing, goals will always be there. Continue to push beyond your limits and reach new heights. You will be amazed at how much you can accomplish when you know what direction you are going in.

Overtraining

I mentioned earlier about overtraining and how it can have a negative impact on an athlete. This is one of the biggest enemies of a fighter because it feels like you can't train enough. Also, every moment you are not training, someone else is. As a result, you get left behind.

Overtraining can actually do more harm than good and lead to many long-term issues for a boxer. Some of the signs to look out for are:

- Not enjoying the sport.
- Being obsessed about training nonstop to the point it takes over your life.
- Chronic pain and muscle fatigue.
- Loss of appetite.
- Increased heart rate at rest.
- Frequent illnesses.
- Difficulty recovering from injuries.
- Decreased performance in the sport.
- Negative mood changes.
- Sleep disturbances.

My goal with this book was to introduce you to boxing and make it fun for you. Unfortunately, it will have the opposite effect if you overtrain and even lead to chronic illnesses in the future. For example, overtraining can put excessive strain on the heart, cause undue damage to the muscles, and cause severe injuries. Too much muscle breakdown can lead to problems with other internal organs, including the heart.

It is essential to work hard and progress with your training. However, you need to listen to your body, and if it is telling you something is wrong, you must take it seriously. Give yourself ample time to recover, especially after an injury. If you had a tough competition or workout session in the gym, it is okay to take a day off if needed. Make training fun for you. Do not move faster than you feel comfortable. For example, if you train for 30 minutes on day one, don't jump to an hour the next day. Move up slowly until you reach this goal.

My hope is that you fall in love with boxing and make it a lifelong activity. In order for this to occur, you must always enjoy it. For this reason alone, I do not want you to overtrain. It will not be beneficial for you to do so.

Chapter 7: #7 Additional Defensive Techniques and How to Return a Punch

Your offense is what will ultimately win you fights. However, your defense is what prevents you from losing them. All of the greats in the past had their own way of defending against strikes. They could hit and not get hit, whether they were aggressive fighters or more counterpunchers.

If you study fighters like Muhammad Ali, Mike Tyson, Lennox Lewis, Bernard Hopkins, Roy Jones, Jr., or Floyd Mayweather, you will notice that they have different styles, but all were great at defending against their opponents' assault. Some of them made it look like a work of art.

I discussed defensive techniques in part one of this book but will get into more detail here. No matter how good you get at offense, never forget about your defensive skills. Not only will it help win fights, but you will avoid damage that will take its toll over time.

Layers of Defense

The layers of defense refer to the different areas of your body that can be utilized for defensive tactics based on what your opponent is doing. Whether your opponent is stalking you, backtracking, throwing body blows, or headhunting, you can use the different layers of defense to keep yourself protected. Remember that whatever method you use, keep your opponent in front of you and never take your eyes off them. If you lose sight of your opponent, you will get hit by that unforeseen punch. The following are the different layers of defense:

- Defending with the hands. Your hands are the first layer of defense, so hold them up and use them to maintain distance, and block, catch or parry any punch thrown towards the head. Make your movements with your hands quickly so you can move them back into position to defend against other strikes.
- Defending with the arms and elbows. Once your opponent closes the distance, they can start landing body blows. Your arms and elbows can be used for the second layer of defense. As your opponent throws punches to the body, block them by keeping your arms and elbows near you. When you see an opportunity, you can quickly tie them up.

- Defending with the feet is the third layer of defense. This mostly relates to footwork and how well you can move around the ring and keep your opponent guessing. The objective here is not to get trapped, so keep circling, backpedaling, shifting, skipping, or walking the ring.
- Defending with the shoulders is another way to avoid shots to the head. This is the fourth layer of defense. As your opponent throws a punch, roll your shoulder in the same direction. The strike will roll off the shoulder rather than landing on the head. From this position, you can throw a counter strike, like an uppercut or a hook.
- The fifth and final layer of defense is drawing a line in the sand. This is used to play mind games on your opponent. As you stand in front of your opponent, draw an imaginary line on the ground. If

your opponent crosses it, you can perform various tactics, like crouch down low to signal an attack or stand up straight to invite an attack, effectively setting a trap. You can use multiple methods to manipulate your opponent from here. If they do throw a strike, you can counter it.

As you can see, there are many aspects of the defense game that you need to be aware of. Practice these defensive tactics during your sparring and mitt work sessions.

Boxing Guards

There are a variety of different guards that boxers use. I will go over some of the most well-known and effective methods to help you become a great defensive fighter:

The Philly Shell Guard

This defensive guard was perfected masterfully by Floyd Mayweather, Jr. Start by getting into a wider stance with your less dominant side forward. Your lead hand is kept a little low to protect you from body shots. The lead shoulder is kept high to help deflect punches by rolling them off this shoulder. The rear hand is held high to protect against lead hooks.

The Peek-a-Boo Guard

Mike Tyson made this guard famous in his prime. You keep your hands high, hugging your head. The stance will be square so you can hit with equal power on both sides. Stay low with your knees bent. Mike Tyson was effective with this method because of his constant head movement from side-to-side and his ability to roll and duck under punches. The 1st photo shows the normal peek-a-boo guard while the other two photos show how to slip punches while in that guard.

Mexican Style Guard

This style was made famous by many Mexican fighters, like Marco Antonio Barrera. With this style, you will keep your rear arm in a traditional position with the handheld high next to the head. The shoulder should also be tucked in for extra protection. The lead hand will be held out in front and move in a rhythmic fashion to block and parry an opponent's punches.

Drunken Boxer Guard

This last guard is probably the most difficult and should only be used by advanced boxers. With this stance, you will hold your hands down low near your waist. It will appear like you are wide open; however, this is just a trap. The boxer using this method will rely heavily on head movement, footwork, slips, and parries. They can often get their opponents to overcommit and unleash a fury of punches. Boxers like Prince Naseem Hamed and Roy Jones, Jr. made this guard famous. No photo included, just simply because you will constantly be using your hands to parry in fights, and I am sure you know how to hold your hands near your waist.

Countering Different Punches

When you start sparring, you will be surprised at how difficult it is to create openings with a moving target. If they are trained, their guard will always be up too, which makes it even more difficult. Your opponent's defense is the most open when they are throwing a punch, which means this is the best opportunity to hit them with your counterpunch.

This is a difficult technique to master, but also one of the most important. When you throw a counterpunch, you are also leaving yourself open, too, so you need to make sure that any strike you throw lands. I will go over the most common punches used in boxing and the best way to counter them.

Jab

There are a number of ways to counter a jab. The first thing you can do is block the jab with your right glove and throw a counter jab right back at them. Keep the shoulder of your jab hand high, and your chin tucked in case they throw a right cross after the jab. When you throw the jab, go directly for your opponent's face or chin.

You can bend your knees and lower your body to duck their jab while throwing a counter jab to their body. From here, you can throw a right cross to the head. You can also lean your head slightly inside of their left arm as he throws a jab and counter with a slightly arched right cross.

Finally, you can use the parry. As they throw a jab, you can parry the punch down with your right or dominant hand and then fire a straight right over their parried arm. They will be wide open at this point.

Right Cross

As your opponent throws a right cross, you can thwart the attack with a quick left jab to the head. Make sure to hold your left shoulder high to avoid getting hit by the right cross. You can also block the punch with your left hand and immediately throw a right to the head. A counter right cross would make the most sense here.

Wide Right Hook

As your opponent's hand leaves his chin, you can immediately counter with a short-left hook. As you throw this punch, turn your body clockwise, so your head turns away from the right hook. Even if the right hook lands, it won't be as forceful. Just make sure your left hook finds its target.

Baiting Your Opponent

The most straightforward punches to counter are the ones that you see coming. So, either your opponent telegraphs their strikes, or you can set up a trap by baiting them. Basically, don't wait for your opponent to punch, but force them to punch. In a fight, you do not have time to wait for opportunities. You must create them. A common method is to bait your opponent, so they fall for your trap. You can do this by pretending they have an opening. When they execute the punch, you wanted them to throw, you can counter with your own strike.

An example of this is to lower your glove a few inches while slightly leaning your head back. Your opponent will think you are open when in reality, you are even more guarded. Do not go overboard here and drop your hands completely to taunt your opponent. I don't care how many times Roy Jones, Jr. has done it. I don't want you to be this careless. Let's go over some ways to bait your opponent into throwing specific punches.

Jab

Lower your hands slightly while standing at a distance. Only your opponent's jab should be able to reach you. As they see your head uncovered, they will throw that jab. You need to be prepared to close the distance and counter when they do. As you move your head, you can throw a counter jab, a right cross, or even a lunging left hook if you are quick enough.

Right Hand

You can throw a lazy jab or simply hold out your left glove. Your opponent is likely to counter with a right hand. You need to be ready to slip the punch when they throw it and throw your own right-hand counter. You can also throw a left hook. Some experienced fighters will bait the right hand by leaning slightly forward to close the range. They will pull their head back once the punch is thrown, and then you can counter.

Left Hook

To bait the left hook, you can throw a soft 1-2 combination. You can also move into close range. After the left hook is thrown, be ready to roll under it and counter with an uppercut or your own short hook.

Body Shot

Stand at a long-range and expose your mid-section. Once your opponent throws a jab to the body, which is the most likely punch to reach that distance, you can counter with a right hand. You can bait body shots at close range by pulling your opponent's head or shoulders down.

Southpaw Left Cross

Throw a combination at your opponent, like a jab-right cross combo and wait for the counter left cross. Be ready to slip the punch and counter with a right to the head or body.

Forcing the Counter

A more aggressive way to make your opponent throw a punch is by forcing them. This way, you do not have to wait for them to create an opportunity for you. You are making one yourself. Move forward and hit your opponent with everything you have until they fight back. Once they do, counter their punches. Let's go over some ways to force specific punches.

The Jab

Stay at long range and continuously stuff a jab in your opponent's face while continually moving your head. Eventually, they will throw a jab to reach you, and you can counter from here.

The Right Hand

Keep throwing jabs at your opponent. Be close enough that he can reach you with a straight right hand, but not a left hook. You can also circle towards your opponent's right to make them think they have a good opening. From here, slip his punch and counter with your own right. You can close the distance and throw an uppercut and hook too.

The Left Hook

Get closer to your opponent's right hand and smother it. Take away room for them to throw a right, so they will be forced to throw a left hook. This punch is instinctive when fighting at close range. Once the left hook is thrown, roll under it and counter with a right, or your own left hook.

Southpaw Left

If your opponent is a southpaw, move towards their left hand while throwing rights at them. Make sure you keep yourself out of distance from his right hook, so he will be forced to throw a big left cross. Slip to the outside and throw your own right cross. You can also force the left cross by throwing rights at his glove.

With all of the defensive techniques I have gone over in this chapter, I advise that you train with a partner, whether it be mitt drills, sparring, or both. You need to learn how to perform these maneuvers when actual punches are being thrown at you. one on one training with a partner, or several, will vastly improve all your defensive skills.

Chapter 8: How to Successfully Take Your Skills to the Ring

Once again, we are at a fork in the road, and it is time for you to decide which direction you want to go. Whatever you choose, I just hope you plan to stick with boxing for the rest of your life. It is a great workout and extremely fun to do. The skills you learn with boxing are not just exclusive to the sport but will help you in every aspect of your life. You will become more disciplined, focused, healthy, and goal-oriented. You will never wonder again what a good workout regimen is. Every time you perform these drills, you will feel like you're getting more fit.

With the information I have provided in this book, you will have a competitive edge in the boxing world. From here, you can continue to build your skills and start competing against other pugilists in your weight class. However, the ball is in your court. If you decide not to compete and just continue working the drills, that is good enough for me. I am just glad to have exposed all of you to a sport that I have loved and been a part of for years. I have taken you as far as I will go, and it's your time to take the ball and run with it. For this final chapter, I will discuss how you can advance in this sport if you decide to do so.

Getting Involved in Competition

Once you are ready to start competing, there are several steps you need to take. The first thing you need to do is get into incredible shape. You can start doing many of the drills and exercises at home; however, you will eventually need to find a boxing gym or personal boxing trainer. It is necessary to work out on the heavy bags, get guidance from a coach, and feel what it's like to be in a boxing ring. Make sure you understand the difference between a boxing gym that trains you for competition versus a gym dedicated to cardio fitness. Cardio boxing will get you in shape but not ready for competition.

The coach or trainer at the gym can start teaching you various techniques and have you hit the punching bags. They can also start having you shadowbox in the ring. After you get used to these methods, you can move over to mitt drills. These exercises will work on your punching techniques, reflexes, footwork, defensive skills, and other fight game areas. Once you are ready, you can start sparring with an opponent.

You will need to get an amateur boxing license by first passing a physical. Try finding a physician who specializes in physicals for boxers or combat athletes. Obtain a signed copy of the physical and fill out an application with USA boxing. If you live outside the US, find out what your governing body is for amateur boxing. Send whatever they request with the application, like a copy of your birth certificate. There will be a registration fee for your local boxing committee.

Once your application is cleared, you can start signing up for competition. Your coach or trainer can advise you on when you're adequately trained. Competitions are broken down by weight class. When you start, you will compete on the local circuit. From here, you can advance to state and national competitions when you are ready. Some amateurs even compete on the international levels.

The Golden Gloves are the highest-ranking national titles an amateur can win in the US. On the international front, the World Championships and Olympics are the highest levels of competition. Of course, it takes years of training and competition to get to this spot. If any of you make it to the Olympics because I inspired you to start boxing, it will be a great honor for me.

While this book does provide great information, you still need to find a coach at your local boxing gym. They can give you more personalized attention to hone your skills and make you competition ready. If you are part of a boxing gym, there will be plenty of students to train with, as well. You can have many different sparring partners.

What to Look For in a Boxing Coach

Muhammad Ali had Angelo Dundee. Mike Tyson had Kevin Rooney. Roberto Duran had Ray Arcel. Behind every great boxer was a trainer who helped hone their skills. When you look for a coach yourself, you should follow a particular set of criteria, especially if your goal is to compete down the line. Of course, you want to make sure there is good chemistry. When you are struggling and in the fight of your life, you are going to be happy that you chose who would be in your corner wisely. The following are some of the significant factors you should consider when looking for a boxing coach:

- The coach should have a lot of experience, either by fighting in the ring, coaching many different fighters, or both.

- They should be organized and prepared. If your coach is failing to prepare, they are preparing to fail. The person they will be failing is you. Your coach must have a plan for development and progress that both of you should agree on. If the lessons are loosely-structured with no real plan, that is not a good sign.
- They should be attentive to detail so they can determine your strengths and weaknesses. This comes from years of assessing various fighters and styles.
- A good coach will motivate you to keep going. They will be firm but not abusive. You do not have to take insults or be bullied.
- They should have good communication skills and impart knowledge in a way that is understandable for you.

Communication also means they will listen to what you have to say and respond appropriately.

- The coach will see you as part of their team and not some subordinate they can look down on.
- They should be optimistic about your future and success-oriented.
- They have good character and are completely upfront with you.
- I don’t want you to break the bank here, so price is definitely a factor.

While you are the one who will ultimately step in the ring to compete, a good trainer will be your guiding light. They will support you, encourage you, constantly update the game plan based on what is happening, give you strategic advice, and so much more. You can tell when a fighter's corner does not know what they are doing, and it is a sad sight to witness.

Start Your Goal Setting

Once you decide to start training, let the goal-setting begin. Even if you don't end up competing, you can still set fitness goals for yourself. I encourage you to create boxing-related goals, like when you want to compete, how many rounds you want to spar each week, deadlines for weight loss and how much, or how many different punches do you want to learn.

Here are some examples of boxing goals:

- Being able to shadow box for three, two-minute rounds by the end of the first week in the gym.
- Having your first sparring session within 30 days.
- Competing in your first tournament after six months.

- After competing at the local level for a while, competing at the state level at the one-year mark.

The goals you create need to be precise with a specific deadline. Do not make general statements like:

- I will box someday.
- I hope to spar eventually.
- I will work out on the heavy bag when I am comfortable.

These are not good goals because they lack any real substance or urgency. Whenever you come up with a goal, always remember the acronym SMART, which stands for:

- Specific: You must know precisely what you want.

- Measurable: There needs to be a way to track your progress.
- Attainable: It should be a realistic goal.
- Relevant: It should pertain to whatever you are doing.
- Time-bounded: There should be a deadline.

When you start setting goals for your boxing workouts, you can use the same approach for your personal life. The various philosophies that bring success in the squared-circle can also apply to all other areas of our lives. For example, the discipline and focus to attain from boxing can also be used in your career or relationships.

Boxing is a Metaphor for Life

Boxing is a metaphor for life in some specific ways. Many of the common phrases you hear, like, “roll with the punches” or “stick and move,” originated from the world of combat sports. Here are a few more ways that boxing relates to real life:

- You get what you put in: When it comes down to the wire, the winner is often the one who did the most work beforehand. This means the one who did the most roadwork, drills, and sparring, etc. In the real world, winners are also decided by who put in the most effort.
- Respect is earned, not given: Both in the ring and in everyday life, respect is not handed over on a silver platter. It is earned through the right actions. Of course, in our regular lives, it is generally received when we do something noble. In boxing, it is received when we punch someone in the face.

- Having a strong corner: Every great fighter had a strong corner to support them through good and bad times. The same is necessary for life. No matter how independent we are, we need a good support system to guide us.
- Throwing in the towel: In the ring, sometimes we are too overwhelmed, and there is no hope. We must throw in the towel. In life, we must also occasionally throw in the towel when it comes time to cut our losses and reorganize for the next opportunity.
- Low blows: In the ring, a low blow occurs when a punch is physically thrown below the belt. These low blows usually come in the form of negative comments, insults, cheap shots, or backstabbing in life. We must be aware of these low blows and be prepared to recover from them in any event.

Your Free Gift

The gift you will receive is “The Basic Boxing Bundle”. In this bundle you will find many ‘extras’ that will help you improve your boxing ability in many ways. In this bundle you will find...

An equipment checklist – a page that has all the equipment mentioned in this book in a list with a link to where you can find it for a reasonable price on a website. Although all the equipment is not needed it certainly will help you improve.

Secondly, you will find 5 Boxing Drills that you can complete at home. Each drill is different to help develop certain aspects of your boxing game, one thing they all have in common is that they get you working hard. The drills are detailed and essential for improvement.

Finally, you will find a Boxing Video Hub. I believe that these videos are helpful for learning correct form and each video in the Hub is labelled so that you know what boxing video you are clicking on.

Follow this link:

https://hudsonandrew.activehosted.com/f/1

Join the Chump to Champ Community

Boxing on your own is difficult because it requires you to motivate yourself to train on a regular basis, motivating yourself is much more challenging that having a coach shout in your ear to finish your reps. Training on your own is very beneficial because it allows you to make the training specific to you so that you can work on your own schedule and improve the parts of your boxing that suits your style. That's why you should join the Chump to Champ Community.

In this Free Facebook Community, you will be able to discover much more information about boxing because I post twice a day. These posts consist of beginner information, debunking myths, providing links to videos for your benefit, many boxing trivia questions and so much more for your entertainment and benefit. Not to mention there are many other members in this community in your position, anyone can contribute in any way they like and if you join please make a post about yourself to feel welcomed by the other members

Follow this link to join the Chump to Champ Community:
https://www.facebook.com/groups/chumptochamp

Conclusion

Well, here we are. You made it to the end of part 2 of my book, *Boxing: From Chump to Champ 2*. I hope that both books' combined information has provided you with the knowledge and inspiration to take up boxing as a regular sport. Whether you decide to compete or simply use the drills and exercises to get a good workout, there is a wealth of knowledge you can start incorporating into your daily routine right away.

Boxing is a challenging sport, both mentally and physically. However, the benefits you receive are priceless, both in sport and everyday life. As you read through the chapters of this book, I hope you could determine how to advance on your boxing skills and further your training. The variety of drills provided are meant to be used in many different settings. Once you get into better shape with general exercises, you can start going to a boxing gym and focusing more on drills related to the sport.

My advice is to engage in all of the drills I went over, from shadowboxing, heavy bag work, and sparring, plus all of the other mentioned exercises. Including all of these drills into your routine will cover every aspect of your boxing game. Also, your boxing coach or trainer will be able to give you personalized attention to help develop your technique and skills. You will benefit immensely from one on one training in both your offensive and defensive maneuvers.

If you plan to compete someday, you will have to do a lot of sparring, as I discussed in the book. Sparring is the final preparation before any competition. Shadowboxing, mitt work, hitting the heavy bag, and performing any other drill I mentioned will be helpful, but you will never know how good you are until there is a moving target in the ring who is trying to hit you back. Sparring will allow you to practice every aspect of your game in a real-life situation.

No matter what direction you decide to go, I will support your decision. I want you to love the sport of boxing, and my hope is that it will help you as much as it did me. Always remember to have fun, stay relaxed, work hard, but don't overtrain. The last thing I want is for you to fall in love with boxing, only to lose your enthusiasm for it.

I urge you to use this book as a manual that you can reference frequently. If you have forgotten some of the basics from part one, then refer back to that one too. Boxing will be a lifelong journey for you, and you will find many parallels to life the more you get involved. For example, goal-setting is a major factor for success in the squared circle, just like it is in real life.

Now that you have completed this book and have the necessary tools for success in the sweet science, it is time to start taking action. Take the information I have provided and begin adding it to your routine. If you haven't already, start checking out the local boxing gyms in your area. Find the one that you feel is the best fit for you. If you love boxing, don't wait any longer to get started. You will begin getting in shape in no time while building confidence.

My Books

The Chump to Champ Collection

Circuit Training for Weight Loss

References

Dec Beales - Model for the Exercise Demonstrations. https://www.instagram.com/dec.beales/

Your Free Gift – The Basic Boxing Bundle. https://hudsonandrew.activehosted.com/f/1

Join the Facebook Community. https://www.facebook.com/groups/chumptochamp

Follow my Facebook Page. https://www.facebook.com/andrewhudsonbooks1

Email me for extra support. andrew@hudsonandrew.com

8 Limbs. (2017, May 4). *How to increase your punching speed.* Eightlimbs. https://eightlimbs.com.au/increase-punching-speed/

Beasley, C. (n.d.). *3 Tips to Develop a Champion's Mindset*. Retrieved November 14, 2020, from https://fightcampconditioning.com/mindset-for-mma/

Boxing Inc. (2017, November 13). *4 Important (and Smart) Reasons to Give Personal Training a Try*. Boxing Inc. https://boxingincorporated.com/4-important-smart-reasons-give-personal-training-try/

Brightside. (2019). *7 Exercises for Men to Build a Big Strong Neck*. YouTube. https://youtu.be/I1ertAfrClU

Chan, J. (2017). 7 Benefits to fighting with hands LOW [YouTube Video]. In *YouTube.* https://www.youtube.com/watch?v=A8XzdCg5r4M

Cottonbro. (n.d.). *Silhouette of 2 Person Standing in Front of a Mirror.* https://www.pexels.com/photo/silhouette-of-2-person-standing-in-front-of-a-mirror-4761616/

Cunningham, S. (2019, May 28). *Boxing Drills: Agility Training for Boxing*

Footwork. Ringside Boxing Blog. https://blog.ringside.com/boxing-footwork-agility-training/

Dawson, Al. (n.d.). *How To Keep Your Gas In A Boxing Match | Nutaofit Martial Arts*. Nutaofit Martial Arts. Retrieved November 14, 2020, from https://www.nutaofitmartialarts.com/how-to-keep-your-gas-in-a-boxing-match/

Dawson, A. (2018, April 23). *This is everything boxing champion Floyd Mayweather eats and drinks for breakfast, lunch, and dinner*. Business Insider Australia. https://www.businessinsider.com.au/what-floyd-mayweather-eats-drinks-2018-4

Diranian, S. (n.d.). *How to Get Started in Amateur Boxing*. LIVESTRONG.COM. Retrieved November 14, 2020, from https://www.livestrong.com/article/420913-how-to-get-started-in-amateur-boxing/

Evolve MMA. (2018, February 9). *4 Ways To Fortify Your Midsection And*

Protect Yourself From Body Shots - Evolve Daily. Evolve MMA Singapore. https://evolve-mma.com/blog/4-ways-to-fortify-your-midsection-and-protect-yourself-from-body-shots/

Evolve MMA. (2018b, August 18). *How To Use The Clinch Effectively In Boxing - Evolve Daily*. Evolve MMA Singapore. https://evolve-mma.com/blog/how-to-use-the-clinch-effectively-in-boxing/

Fairytale, E. (n.d.). *Women Practicing Yoga*. https://www.pexels.com/photo/women-practicing-yoga-3822195/

fightTIPS. (2015). 10 Advanced Sparring Tips for MMA, Boxing, & Muay Thai [YouTube Video]. In *YouTube*. https://www.youtube.com/watch?v=Nko2GqifUAw&list=PLeTqmYY-B2OPw_cK1__7hCyuMtCVXSVoW&index=7&t=0s

fightTIPS. (2019). 4 Styles of Boxing Guards [YouTube Video]. In *YouTube*. https://www.youtube.com/watch?v=AJWu7TCwGTo

Fissori, B. (2018, September 10). *Eat Like a Boxer: Standard Boxer Diet - Boxing Insider*. BoxingInsider.com. https://www.boxinginsider.com/weight-loss/eat-like-a-boxer-standard-boxer-diet/

Gloveworx. (2020, January 7). *The Art of Shadowboxing | Why We Shadowbox*. Gloveworx. https://www.gloveworx.com/blog/shadowboxing-part-one/#:~:text=Shadowboxing%20is%20a%20training%20method

Gonchare, M. (n.d.). https://www.pexels.com/photo/healthy-man-people-woman-4348626/

Ha, S. (2013, January 25). *Boxing Masterclass - How to Beat a Pressure Fighter*. MightyFighter.com - Boxing Training | Fitness | Motivation. https://www.mightyfighter.com/how-to-beat-a-pressure-fighter/

Ha, S. (2013b, February 4). *Top 9 Methods on How to Take a Punch*. MightyFighter.com - Boxing Training | Fitness | Motivation.

https://www.mightyfighter.com/top-9-methods-on-how-to-take-a-punch/

Ha, S. (2013c, March 4). *Top 5 Advanced Boxing Techniques.* MightyFighter.com - Boxing Training | Fitness | Motivation. https://www.mightyfighter.com/top-5-advanced-boxing-techniques/

Law of the Fist. (n.d.). *13 Ways to Improve Your Fighting Reflexes – Law Of The Fist*. Law of the Fist. Retrieved November 13, 2020, from https://lawofthefist.com/13-ways-to-improve-your-fighting-reflexes/

Leunen, S. (n.d.). *Strong Man Training in Modern Gym.* https://www.pexels.com/photo/strong-man-training-in-modern-gym-5496589/

Mindful Staff. (2019, January 31). *How to Meditate - Mindful*. Mindful. https://www.mindful.org/how-to-meditate/

Moss, P. (2016, September 1). *5 Reasons Why The Sport of Boxing Is A Metaphor For Life*. Boxing News and Views.

https://www.boxingnewsandviews.com/2016/09/01/boxing-is-a-metaphor-for-life/

N, J. (2009, July 2). *7 Easy Boxing Counters*. How to Box | ExpertBoxing. https://expertboxing.com/7-easy-boxing-counters-punches

N, J. (2010, November 2). *7 Basic Boxing Combinations*. How to Box | ExpertBoxing. https://expertboxing.com/7-basic-boxing-combinations

N, J. (2011, August 27). *Baiting and Forcing Counters*. How to Box | ExpertBoxing. https://expertboxing.com/baiting-and-forcing-counters

N, J. (2016, July 27). *7 BEST Boxing Focus Mitt Drills*. How to Box | ExpertBoxing. https://expertboxing.com/7-best-boxing-focus-mitt-drills

N, J. (2019, December 11). *4 BASIC Boxing Footwork Drills*. How to Box | ExpertBoxing.

https://expertboxing.com/basic-boxing-footwork-drills

Overtraining Syndrome/Burnout. (n.d.). Www.Rchsd.org. Retrieved November 14, 2020, from https://www.rchsd.org/programs-services/sports-medicine/conditions-treated/overtraining-syndromeburnout/#:~:text=Burnout%2C%20or%20overtraining%20syndrome%2C%20is

Performance U. (2014). How to do Mountain Climbers Exercise the RIGHT way. [YouTube Video]. In *YouTube.* https://www.youtube.com/watch?v=De3Gl-nC7IQ

Raina, K. (2019, March 8). *10 Exercises That Help You to Increase Your Stamina & Strength.* Parenting.Firstcry.com. https://parenting.firstcry.com/articles/magazine-10-best-exercise-to-increase-stamina-and-strength/

Razzetti, G. (2019, February 8). *21 Simple Mindfulness Exercises to Cope with 2020 Challenges.* Liberationist - Change Leadership.

https://liberationist.org/21-simple-mindfulness-exercises-to-improve-your-focus/

Reemus. (2016, August 29). *Combination Drills For The Heavy Bag*. Reemus Boxing. http://reemusboxing.com/combination-drills-heavy-bag/

Ringside Boxing. (2018, August 25). *Boxing Training for Beginners: How to Train Like a Professional.* Ringside Boxing Blog. https://blog.ringside.com/boxing-training-for-beginners-how-to-train-like-a-professional/

Ringside Boxing. (2019a, January 14). *Boxing Training | 9 Exercises that Will Improve Punching Power | Ringside Blog*. Ringside Boxing Blog. https://blog.ringside.com/9-exercises-improve-punching-power/

Ringside Boxing. (2019a, November 10). *Focus on Fighting Styles, Part 3 - The Slugger | Ringside Boxing*. Ringside Boxing Blog. https://blog.ringside.com/slugger-fighting-style/

Ringside Boxing. (2019, December 9). *Focus on Fighting Styles, Part 4 - The Boxer-Puncher | Ringside Boxing*. Ringside Boxing Blog. https://blog.ringside.com/boxer-puncher-fighting-style/

Samkov, I. (n.d.). *Man Doing Push-Ups*. https://www.pexels.com/photo/man-doing-push-ups-4162491/

Samkov, I. (n.d.-b). *Man in Gray Tank Top Doing Squats*. https://www.pexels.com/photo/man-in-gray-tank-top-doing-squats-4164465/

Sands, F. (n.d.). *Shadow Boxing – 7 Tips for Success*. Www.Myboxingcoach.com. Retrieved November 7, 2020, from https://www.myboxingcoach.com/shadow-boxing/

Sands, F. (2019). *Shadow Boxing - How to Shadow Box - 7 Steps for the Beginner*. YouTube. https://youtu.be/Gl8hF4TbHn8

Sands, F. (2019, December 22). *Boxing Training – 7 Shifts of Attack*. Www.Myboxingcoach.com. https://www.myboxingcoach.com/boxing-training-7-shifts-of-attack/

Stewart, J. (2015, October 3). *35 Boxing Sparring Tips for Beginners*. Warrior Punch. https://warriorpunch.com/35-boxing-sparring-tips-for-beginners/

Walker, D. (2019, February 14). *What Makes a Good Boxing Trainer: A Complete Guide*. WBCME. https://www.wbcme.co.uk/ringside/what-makes-a-good-boxing-trainer/

WikiHow, & Griffin, T. (2006, November 15). *Set Goals*. WikiHow; wikiHow. https://www.wikihow.com/Set-Goals

Printed in Great Britain
by Amazon